Susan,

I hope my stories inspire you to share stories of your own.

Find Your Way Back

How to Write Your Way through Anything

ESSAYS

By
Javacia Harris Bowser

see jane write

FIND YOUR WAY BACK

Printed in the United States of America.

Photo by Melissa Newton of J&M Photography

ISBN: 978-0-578-36528-2

Table of Contents

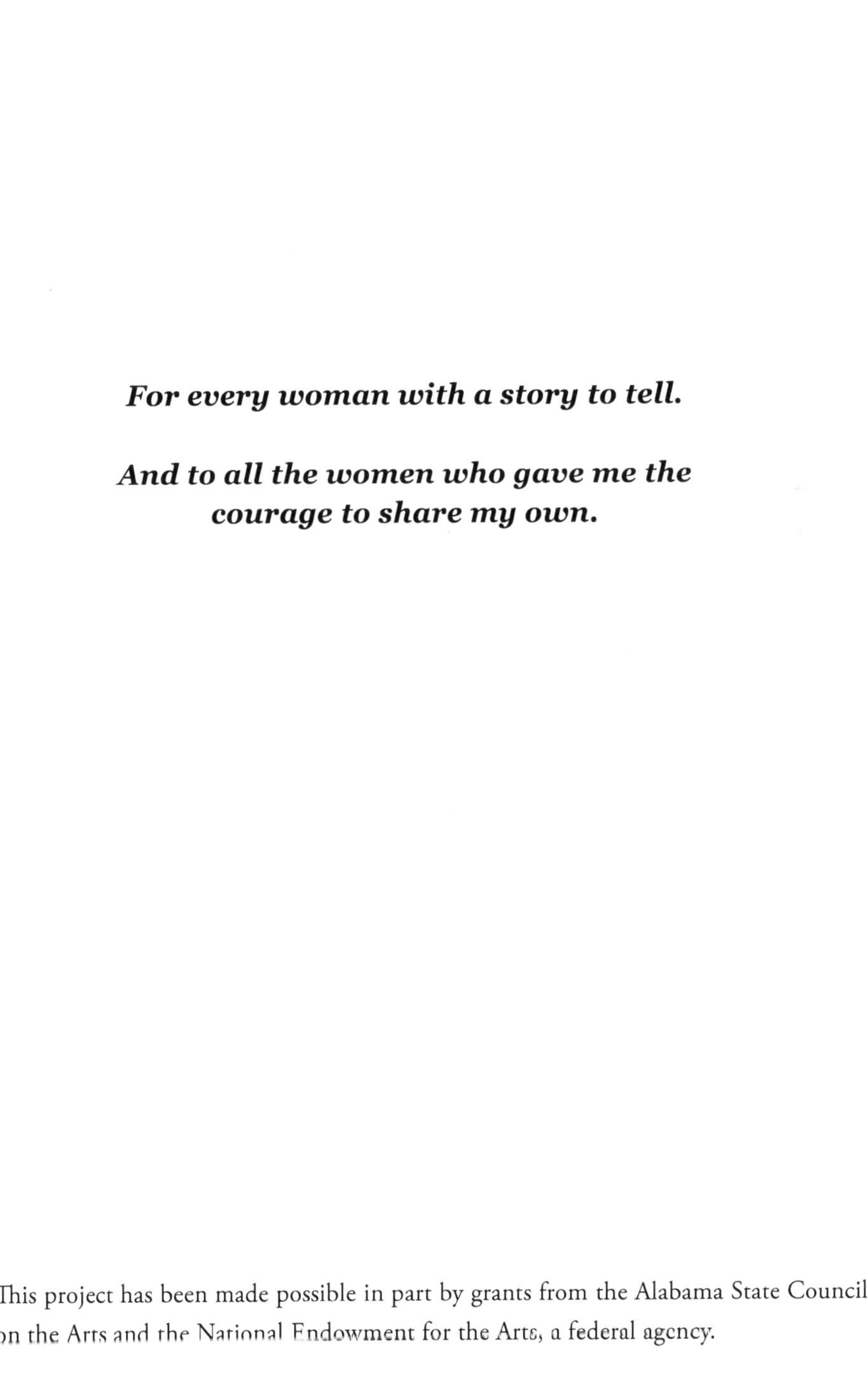

For every woman with a story to tell.

And to all the women who gave me the courage to share my own.

This project has been made possible in part by grants from the Alabama State Council on the Arts and the National Endowment for the Arts, a federal agency.

Foreword

The first day I ever wrote anything even remotely cancer-related was a cold, grey February afternoon in 2012. I sat working at my laptop in a pleasantly warm coffee shop while my husband was home with our young daughter. We had a system down by then: I worked the first part of the day - I was a conference producer working from California for a New York-based firm - and he worked the second half of the day in a local library. We'd become a lot like two ships passing, our daughter our go-between. I was grateful for the opportunity to sneak away from the house and work in the peaceful buzz of the coffee shop. At home, I couldn't help but work with one ear listening to my daughter's faraway squawks and cries, my breasts achingly interpreting each noise she made as a need to nurse.

But on this day, while I should have been inviting insurance executives to speak at a Medicare-related conference, I kept finding myself staring out the window, nervous thoughts tumbling around in my head. I'd just had my first mammogram and ultrasound, and the radiologist had ordered me back for a biopsy of the hard lump I'd discovered one night while breastfeeding. It was a week before my 35th birthday.

Unable to concentrate on work, I opened a blank page on my blog and began to write. I wrote about the night I found the lump, how when I asked my husband to feel it, the blood left his face, and his eyes grew large. I wrote about my older, kindly OB-gyn reassuring me that it was probably just a milk-related cyst but also agreed it should be checked out. I wrote about my fear in the middle of my breast ultrasound when the curt technician, looking grave, left me alone in the exam room for nearly an hour. Finally, I wrote about how I spent that hour thinking of my grandmother on my dad's side, who had passed away from metastatic breast cancer when I was 18.

The blog had started as a wedding tool, a place for guests to gather the information they needed to travel to my big day. Then, when my daughter was born, it pivoted to a "mommy blog," becoming a place for me to write about our struggles as well as share little tidbits that I was learning along the way of nurturing another human being. I found it helpful to have a place to work out my challenges in doing something I'd never done before and also give back a little to my new community of new moms.

When the lump came, the blog evolved once more, beginning before I even knew it on that day in the coffee shop. I would go on to be diagnosed with Stage 3c HER2+ breast cancer. The lump turned out to be an aggressive, fast-growing, 7cm tumor that had already spread to my lymph nodes. The day I shared about the lump, mammogram, ultrasound, and biopsy, I opened myself up to accept the healing power of writing. My vulnerability gave me both the opportunity to try to make sense of what was happening, but also allowed others a view into what I was going through. So many responded with their own breast cancer scares. It gave me hope and let me know I wasn't alone.

Fast forward to February 2021. Again, I sat staring at my laptop while my daughter played in another room, but I wasn't alone this time. Before me, the screen was full of ten Zoom squares, each one containing the face of another young woman diagnosed with breast cancer. By this time, I had turned writing into a business. I was in my fifth year of publishing a magazine of personal narratives from the world of young breast cancer and also teaching women how to tell their stories in a way that would provide them with healing and connection. On this day, the class was full of women from all over the world - from Spain, Canada, the United Kingdom, and various far reaches of the United States. We had gathered together to do what I had instinctively done that long-ago day in the coffee shop: to use writing to make sense of our breast cancer diagnoses.

In one square, Zooming in from Birmingham, Alabama, sat Javacia Harris Bowser. She had short, black curly hair, a radiant smile, and the light sparkled just right on her gold eyeshadow. At a time in a global pandemic when most of us were trying to figure out ring lights and webcams, Jai glowed effortlessly through the screen. It wasn't just her physical self, it was her stories, too. Each week when our class met, we wrote from prompts and shared aloud. When Jai shared, her words were achingly personal but also crafted in a way that gave voice to a deep pain that resonated for us all. Each week as she read, the Chat feature on Zoom would fill up with "Yes!" and "OMG, I understand completely!" and "So beautiful!"

Before long, I would learn that, like me, Javacia had been using writing as a healing tool long before breast cancer came along. She'd been reaching for pen and paper for the majority of her life, for all sorts of traumas and challenges, and had also turned it into a career through freelancing and developing the *See Jane Write* community.

Today, it is an honor to be writing the foreword for Javacia's book. In the months since we met in that Zoom room, we've collaborated on an issue of

Wildfire Magazine, and I've gotten to know Jai even better. What I've learned is that she is a kindred spirit, one who understands so deeply the healing power of words and how important it is to inspire others to bring their stories out of their bodies into the world. This is how we heal ourselves from life's major challenges, how our stories heal each other, and how we ultimately find our way home to ourselves.

You're in for a treat. Enjoy this book. Savor it. I know you'll be thinking, "Yes!" and "OMG, I understand completely!" and "So beautiful!" as Jai's words land in your heart and on your soul in a way that is so achingly familiar.

April Johnson Stearns
Founder & Editor-in-Chief, *Wildfire Magazine*
26 August 2021

Introduction

Things could be worse. I could have cancer. That was always my go-to, my retort, and my refrain when I got bad news. When I found out my boyfriend was cheating on me. When I found out I was broke, and my checking account was overdrawn. Even when I found out I had lupus.

But on January 24, 2020, I was diagnosed with breast cancer, and I had no mantra to make me feel better. No, I hadn't found a lump in my breast because I wasn't looking for one. In my mind, breast cancer wasn't something I needed to worry about until I turned forty. And besides, I already had lupus. There was no way God would let me have two life-threatening illnesses, right?

Wrong.

The mammogram I got earlier that month was meant to be a baseline, something I did because my doctor thought I should. But that mammogram led to another one, which led to an ultrasound, which led to a biopsy, which led to a doctor telling me that I had cancer.

"I know this feels like Mount Everest," the doctor said. "But it's not Mount Everest; it's Oak Mountain."

That's a reference you'll only get if you're from my hometown of Birmingham, Alabama, but with that statement, I had my new mantra. I typed those words in the Notes app on my phone as soon as I could. The first few weeks after my diagnosis, I repeated them daily like a prayer. And I prayed that words would get me through this. Since I was a kid, I have believed that words could get me through anything.

This is why I write.

I believe that we have the power to write our way to the life of our dreams. I believe I did exactly that when I used writing to build a business and become my own boss. Cancer showed me that we can write our way through our worst nightmare too. But this isn't really a book about breast cancer. In a way, this is a book about you.

I wrote this book for the girl in you who has always wanted to write and for the woman in you who struggles to find the time or the courage to put her words on paper. That's why you'll find writing prompts sprinkled throughout the pages. I wrote this book to show you that instead of putting writing on the back burner when life gets turned upside down, we should turn to writing to help life make sense again. I wrote this book to show you that you can write your dreams into reality.

Author's Note:

The following essays recount actual life events as truthfully as my memory permits – but keep in mind my memory is trash thanks to cancer treatment. All dialogue is consistent with the character of the person speaking. The names of some individuals have been omitted or changed to respect their privacy (or simply because I couldn't remember them. #chemobrain).

F2020

It's December 31, 2019, New Year's Eve, my favorite holiday. I'm at a 1920s-themed party wearing a faux vintage sequin dress, pearls, and a feather fascinator in my hair. My husband and I are chatting with two of our friends until we hear it. The violin strokes signal that Cash Money Records is about to start taking over for the 99 and the 2000. So, all conversation must cease.

The friends we're talking to are white, so they're confused. They don't know that for Black folks like my husband and me, the first few notes of Juvenile's hit song, "Back That Thang Up," are a universal cue to rush the dance floor. The beat drops and my husband and I dance until we're breathless. The DJ keeps hitting us with tracks we love, so we keep dancing until our knees remind us that I'm almost thirty-nine, and he's been forty for two months.

Despite my achy joints—like nearly everyone else in the room—I'm declaring over hi-hats and bass that 2020 will be my year. But for me, it's not just the vodka talking.

The year 2019 was monumental. After ten years of juggling my day job as a high school English teacher with my side hustles as a freelance writer, blogger, and writing coach, I took the leap to become a full-time writerpreneur and turned my side hustles into my career.

After quitting my teaching job in May of 2019, I spent the second half of the year not only writing but also traveling to do speaking engagements on blogging and personal brand building. In August, I partnered with a media company to provide opportunities for Southern women writers to get published and get paid. In September, I flew to Palm Springs for a retreat for female entrepreneurs. I was living my freelancing dream and helping others do the same. My goals for 2020 were big and bold, and the success of 2019 had me confident I could achieve each one. I wanted to self-publish a book, start a podcast, write for my favorite publications, grow my coaching business, travel, and raise a lot of money for my favorite non-profits.

But less than a month into 2020, I would be diagnosed with breast cancer. Less than ninety days into 2020, the COVID-19 pandemic would bring the world to a standstill. Businesses would close. Most airports would begin to look like ghost towns. And thousands of lives would be lost. By early June, the world at large would finally start to pay attention to another pandemic that Black Americans have been enduring for years—racially motivated police brutality.

Ahmaud Arbery. Breonna Taylor. George Floyd.

Their deaths, and the murders of so many other Black men and women at the hands of police, would spark civil unrest in cities across the country—including my own. Chemotherapy would make me vulnerable to COVID complications so I couldn't participate in any demonstrations. Instead, I would protest with my pockets by donating to organizations supporting the Black Lives Matter movement. And I would protest with my words by encouraging others to do what they could.

By the summer, when I look at pictures of myself from New Year's Eve, I feel as if I don't even know the girl staring back at me. Avenue Beat's "F2020"—which would eventually land at number one on *The New York Times* Best Songs of 2020 list—becomes my anthem.[1] But for a while, I would forget what it feels like to be joyous enough to dance.

I had to flip the script—literally. I had to journal my way back to joy. Scripting is a type of law of attraction journaling technique through which you write the script for your future. You journal about the future you want but in the present tense as if it already exists.

I'd been interested in scripting for a long time. Years ago, I read a Blavity article about writer Octavia Butler stating that Butler "literally wrote her life into existence." In her journals, Butler boldly declared that her novels would be a success, that she would be "a bestselling writer," that her books would be "read by millions of people," and that she would help "poor black youngsters" by broadening their horizons.[2]

Soon Butler's affirmations became her reality. The success of novels like *Mind of My Mind*, *Clay's Ark*, and the widely recognized *Kindred,* landed her on bestseller lists, and she went on to receive many awards and accolades, including a grant from the MacArthur Foundation, a PEN Center West Lifetime Achievement Award, and induction into the Science Fiction Hall of Fame.[2]

Awards and accolades would be nice. But I simply wanted to make it to the end of the year alive and with my joy intact. So, I joined a group coaching program led by master coach and fellow breast cancer survivor Rachel Luna. Through her Faith Activated Journaling Experience, she uses journaling and scripting to help female entrepreneurs grow their businesses and improve their lives. Honestly, I wasn't thinking about my business when I signed up. I just knew I needed something to help me through what was about to be the greatest challenge of my life. So, I began to script. Here's what I wrote on May 16, 2020, just nine days after starting chemotherapy:

2020 could have been the worst year of my life. And at first, I thought it would be because, on January 24, I was diagnosed with breast cancer. Then COVID-19 sent the world into a global health pandemic and economic crisis.

But I began a new journaling practice—one fueled by faith—and I began to trust and rely on God like never before. And as a result, I not only survived a pandemic, cancer, and chemotherapy—I thrived.

During chemotherapy and radiation treatments I was so healthy physically, mentally, emotionally, spiritually, and financially that people around me knew this was a miracle. They knew this was the work of God, and people grew closer to God because of my story.

Instead of chemo brain, I got chemo creativity! Throughout my treatments, I had a flood of ideas for building my business and for essays and stories, and God gave me the strength to bring them to fruition.

I must say I don't believe that the declarations in my journal will come true simply because I wrote them down. Faith without works is dead, right? But there's actually some science behind the idea of the power of affirmations – which is really what scripting is all about. Some psychologists say affirmations work because they urge you to act accordingly.[3] You're not going to declare you're a best selling author every day and then never write a word. Likewise, my journal declarations pushed me to live life to the fullest despite cancer and all going on in the world.

And the funny thing about scripting is it doesn't matter if all the dreams you write come true or not. What matters is that the dreams give you the hope you need to fight another day.

How Does a Feminist Fight Cancer?

I was in my early twenties when I started calling myself a feminist—long before Beyonce's song "***Flawless" made feminism cool. It was in my early twenties that I finally learned that—despite popular opinion—feminism had nothing to do with hating makeup, marriage, or men.

In the song "***Flawless" from Queen Bey's 2013 self-titled album, we're given a clear-cut definition of what being a feminist means courtesy of a snippet from Nigerian writer Chimamanda Ngozi Adichie's TED Talk, "We Should All Be Feminists."[1] Feminist: the person who believes in the social, political, and economic equality of the sexes. Merriam-Webster also defines feminism as "organized activity on behalf of women's rights and interests."[2]

But for me, those definitions only scratch the surface. Yes, I call myself a feminist because I believe in women's rights and the equality of the sexes. But I also call myself a feminist because simply put, I'm obsessed with women, and I'm obsessed with being a woman. That's why as a freelance journalist, I mostly write stories for and about women. That's why in 2011, I started a website and online community for women who write and blog called *See Jane Write*. And that's why I believe in sisterhood—for real.

I feel an inexplicable kinship to nearly every woman on the planet, regardless of her age, race, or religion. It doesn't matter if she's a CEO of a company on the Fortune 500 list or a cashier at my local supermarket struggling to make ends meet. Whether she's a princess or a pole dancer, in my mind, we are inextricably linked.

But after being diagnosed with breast cancer in January of 2020, I found myself wondering if being a woman was as wonderful as I'd always thought it to be. My oncologist told me early on that after chemotherapy and radiation treatments, I would have to take the drug Tamoxifen for five to ten years. The tumor found in and removed from my left breast turned out to be "ER-positive." That means the cancer cells grow in response to the hormone estrogen.

When explaining why I needed medication that would essentially push me into early menopause, my doctor said, "Estrogen tried to kill you." Those words stunned me more than, "You have cancer."

Learning that the thing that makes me a woman—biologically, at least—was the very thing threatening to end my life caused the earth beneath me to shift. As an ally to the trans community, I understand intellectually that gender is much more than biology. But emotionally, I felt betrayed by my body and by my womanhood.

Despite the sexism that women can face at work, home, church, and even while walking down the street, I have never seen being a woman as a cross to bear. Of course, I was aware of the horrific oppression faced by women and girls in some countries—including the United States. But these stories and statistics only made me more fiercely feminist. I wanted every woman to feel like womanhood was a blessing. But now, all of a sudden, it felt like a curse.

For months I tried to keep my diagnosis a secret, only telling a few close family members and friends about the lumpectomy I had in February of 2020. But as I got closer to my first day of chemotherapy, I knew I'd soon have to share the news with more people because soon I'd be bald.

There was no chance I'd run into friends at a networking event or at my favorite restaurant or wine bar. The COVID-19 pandemic had us all confined to our homes. But because of See Jane Write, I do live broadcasts on Facebook, and I post pictures and videos to Instagram often. I knew eyebrows would raise once people noticed I no longer had any. I knew I would have to go public with this fight against cancer, and I knew I would have to fight like a feminist.

But how does a feminist fight cancer? First, she makes a playlist because every battle needs a fight song. Of course, Destiny Child's "Survivor" is at the top of my list.

But just as there's no one way to be a woman, there's no single way to be a feminist. And likewise, every cancer warrior must fight in their own way.

Being a writer, I decided I would fight with words. As a friend of mine, who's also a writer, once said, "I fight with my fingertips." That mindset shifted how I approached every aspect of my battle with cancer.

During cancer treatments, I wrote from my body and for my body. I wrote as if the sentences could replace the locks of hair that fell into the shower after my curls became a casualty of chemo. I wrote as if the syllables could dry my tear-stained face. I wrote and pretended the dark spots on my tongue, fingernails, palms, and the bottoms of my feet were splotches of ink.

I wrote as if adjectives could restore my taste buds, allow me to know spicy, savory, and sweet once again. I wrote as if vowels and consonants could calm my constantly queasy belly. I wrote as if my anecdotes were the antidote for the low blood counts that had my doctor wondering if I'd need a blood transfusion.

I wrote even when hand-foot syndrome made it nearly impossible to hold a pen or touch my fingertips to a keyboard.

I wrote and hoped the cadence of my words would help my heart regain its rhythm. Slow down, I whispered to my dear heart. The doctor said 130 beats per minute is much too fast. They poured poison on you, and you panicked, pumping those chemicals away from yourself as fast as you could. Those chemicals they claim will help keep me alive make me wish I were already dead. But I won't die. Not now, at least. I will keep fighting. I will keep writing. When the radiation treatment took its toll, I wrapped my wounds in words and sought comfort in clauses as if each letter were a blot of balm for those burns.

When facing a disease like cancer, fighting for your life isn't simply about fighting to stay alive. You're not only trying to keep your heart beating from one day to the next. When you feel like cancer is taking away every goal and every dream, you're fighting to remember who you are.

So, I write. With Beyoncé's "Find Your Way Back" playing in my ears, I write in journals, essays, poetry, blog posts, and even in the Notes app of my phone.

I write my way back to myself, and I share my words with my sisters so that they—no matter what battle they're fighting—can write their way home too.

How a Fourth Grade Bully Changed My Life

I was on day three of pretending to be sick. But I wasn't *really* lying to my mama. My stomach actually did hurt. But it was no virus that caused this ache. It was Nikia.

Nikia was the most popular girl in the fourth grade at Woodrow Wilson Elementary School. She was a pretty girl with long hair and light eyes, and she already wore a training bra. All the boys wanted to kiss her under the sliding board on the playground, and all the girls wanted to be her best friend.

She ruled over us all, and like any self-respecting evil queen, Nikia loved to torture and toy with her subjects. Each week she would pick one unsuspecting girl for exile. One girl would be singled out, and all the other girls instructed to ignore her.

I was sure I was safe from such a fate. I wasn't popular like Nikia, but I was smart. I helped Nikia and everybody else with things like book reports and fractions. I couldn't be cast aside. She needed me. They all needed me.

But then it happened. I came to school one day and none of the other girls would speak to me. Some of them wouldn't even look at me! And that's when the stomachache hit. I told Ms. Atkinson I was sick, and because I was a straight-A student and teacher's pet, she didn't think for one second that I was lying. With the teacher's aide now in charge, Ms. Atkinson rushed out of the classroom to call my mom, her red hair flowing behind her looking like the fire that raged in my belly.

Mama was there in twenty minutes to whisk me off to our two-bedroom apartment. And so began three days of *Jem and the Holograms* reruns, soda and saltines, and home remedies from my granny that made me throw up—making my stomach virus lie much more believable. Side note—I still don't understand why Black Southern grandmothers are convinced cod liver oil will cure anything.

Nonetheless, by day three, the jig was up.

"Baby," my Mama said as she sat on my bed and smoothed down my hair that I knew she was dreading to comb after it had been untouched for three days. "You have to go back to school tomorrow."

I burst into tears and told Mama everything as she gently stroked my back. Once I finished my story, Mama wiped my tear-stained face, held my shoulders in her hands, looked at me, and said, "Baby, that girl is dumb. And the other girls going along with this are dumb too. You don't need them. Make some new friends."

She made it sound so easy, but I knew better. I also knew it was time to face my fate as an outcast. So, the night before I returned to school, I loaded up my Pound Puppies backpack with some of my favorite books—The Babysitters Club series and Beverly Cleary's tales of Ramona Quimby. I figured if I would no longer have real friends, I could at least have imaginary ones to keep me company at lunch and on the playground. The next morning, I crawled out of my mom's two-door Nissan Sentra and started to make my way to the front door of the school. But I was stopped by Nikia and a few of my former friends.

"While you were gone, we decided that you could be our friend again," Nikia announced. The girls beside her looked happy and relieved, but I wasn't sure if it was because they missed me or if they needed help with the upcoming spelling test. Three days ago, those words from Nikia would have felt like getting one of those giant million-dollar checks from Publishers Clearing House. But at that moment, something clicked. My mama's grown woman wisdom flooded my fourth-grade brain, and I suddenly knew she was right. *This was dumb*!

"Well, while I was gone, I decided that I don't want to be your friend anymore," I told Nikia. She looked like she'd peed her pants. *How dare a lowly peasant deny and defy the queen*!

Then I turned to the other girls and said, "And you shouldn't want to be her friend either because she's mean!"

Then I walked off, resolved to be alone the rest of my life. I had already started to consider asking my mom if I could wear black every day like the sad white kids on TV.

But then, like a scene from an episode of *Punky Brewster,* something magical happened.

"Hey, Javacia!" I heard one of the girls who'd been with Nikia say. "Wait up!"

They all left Nikia and walked away with me.

Odd Girl Out

I have never fit in. I've always been the odd girl out. Growing up, most of the Black kids said I talked "like a white girl" because my subjects and verbs tend to agree. They thought I was weird because of my undying love for Aerosmith, Meatloaf, and Guns N' Roses.

But had I known many white kids at that age, I probably wouldn't have fit in with them either. My name is Black AF. My skin is a darker shade of brown, so there could be no *Imitation of Life* drama going on here even if I wanted (which I didn't). I also grew up in a neighborhood most white kids were too afraid to step foot in.

But this isn't some sob story about how I spent my childhood eating lunch alone or crouched crying in a corner on the playground. I always had plenty of friends because I learned early on that whoever said, "If you can't beat 'em, join 'em" had it all wrong. My philosophy is this: Don't try to beat 'em or join 'em. Simply ignore them and create a squad of your own.

In middle school, I knew I wasn't going to be accepted in the Pretty Girl Clique, or PGC, as they called themselves. They were the Black girls who also "talked like a white girl" but were accepted anyway because they had boobs and booties that all the boys daydreamed of groping (though they didn't stand a chance). Living up to their name, these girls were beautiful and always sported the latest trends. Even when our school instated uniforms, they found a way to look chic in those too. They were smart enough for teachers to like them but not so smart that they were considered nerds.

I was not a pretty girl. I wore my cousin's hand-me-downs and had no idea what the hell to do with my impossibly thick mane of hair. My mom is a proud, self-proclaimed tomboy who couldn't teach me how to put on makeup or shave my legs.

I wasn't a "pretty girl," but I was the smart girl. I was smart enough to win every award on Awards Day except the Most Improved Award; smart enough that popular boys only talked to me when they wanted help with homework; and smart enough that when a popular boy did actually like me in the eighth grade, he was accused of "scraping the bottom of the social ladder." I was also smart enough to be annoyed by that mixed metaphor.

Being smart became my thing. So I joined forces with other smart Black girls in my school, and we became a clique of our own—no official name or acronym necessary. We eventually did have an acronym—NJHS, as in the National Junior Honor Society. We all got inducted, and this became our nerd badge of courage.

Please don't read this and feel sorry for my nerdy friends or me. We certainly didn't feel sorry for ourselves, and we were no angels. We made fun of the other kids just as much as they probably made fun of us. We called them stupid and joked about how they'd be cleaning our houses one day, which was a pretty shitty thing for me to joke about, considering my mom and Granny cleaned office buildings for a living. I often spent my evenings after school helping them.

My friends and I skipped class just like the so-called bad kids. If a teacher stopped us in the hallway for not having a hall pass, we'd just lie and say we were doing something for the Honor Society. It worked every single time.

Around this time, I became known for something else too–writing. I'd been writing poetry and stories since elementary school. After I attended our city's Young Authors Conference, I started keeping a journal because I decided that's what serious writers did. (I've been keeping one ever since.) In seventh grade one of my teachers was so impressed with one of my short stories that she showed other teachers at school. Word got around that "Javacia is a very talented writer," and the principal asked me to team up with the music teacher to write a new school song. Of course, I said yes because I knew this would be another excuse to skip class. The thought of all the popular kids in school being forced to memorize and sing words that I'd written filled me with diabolical joy.

For high school, I attended the Alabama School of Fine Arts (or ASFA), a special school for kids gifted in the arts, math, and science. If you're thirty-five and up, imagine the school from the TV show *Fame* but with a STEM program. If you're under thirty-five, think *Glee*.

Some of my family members worried about me going to a predominantly white school after being in all-Black inner-city public schools my entire life, but I wasn't concerned. That ASFA acceptance letter was like being welcomed into Hogwarts. ASFA was, and still is, nerd heaven and a weird kid haven. Being accepted by an in-crowd was no one's concern because being a school that had an in-crowd was beneath us.

But going to a school for nerds had its drawbacks–I was no longer the smart kid! Being smart could no longer be my thing because everybody was smart. (Case in point, some of the students in my graduating class made perfect scores on their SATs and went on to study at the likes of Harvard, Stanford, and Brown.)

When the first science test I took at ASFA was graded and returned to me, I saw I'd scored a sixty-five. I handed it back to my teacher and said, "This can't be right. I don't make Ds." She looked at me, smiled, and said, "You do now, baby."

I tried to choke back the tears but failed. Then I looked around the classroom and saw other brown tear-stained faces. Like me, these kids were from public schools where we'd maintained an A average without even really trying. Now we were in a science class that used college textbooks. Failing wasn't an option because students at ASFA must maintain a certain grade point average or else be kicked out of the school.

That's when I knew it was time to squad up.

The same science teacher who crushed my fragile freshman ego helped me find my confidence again. One day she invited all the Black students to meet with her after school to give us some words of encouragement and advice, as well as a call to action to stick together. Some of the kids in this group were struggling just as I was. Some were not. (One of the Black students in our crew was a perfect SAT scorer who went to Stanford.) But we all banded together regardless of GPA.

We eventually would call ourselves "Da Clique" because it was the '90s and because ... why not? And we grew to not just include Black students but any student in our class who wanted extra help or wanted to lend a helping hand. We studied together for math, science, and European history tests. We helped one another with essays for English class—the only time I could feel smart again—and through high school heartbreak too. We had annual Christmas parties, complete with Secret Santa, which we continued into adulthood. We took group photos at senior prom. We all graduated, most of us with honors, and, of course, we celebrated together the night after we walked across the stage to receive our diplomas.

Find your people. Whether you do so through networking events in your town or a Facebook group for one of your hobbies – find your people. At work, at church, and every place in between, find your people. You will discover that the things that make you feel lonely or different often are the things that can spark friendships that will last a lifetime. Find your people, and you will never feel like the odd girl out again.

The Sisterhood of the Traveling Pens

Find your people. These are the words I whisper to myself whenever I find myself someplace new. In college, I joined forces with other girls who knew sorority life wasn't for them. In graduate school, I found my people among poets. And when I started working at a weekly newspaper in Louisville, Kentucky, the other women at my paper became some of my best friends.

When I returned to my hometown of Birmingham in 2009 to teach English at the Alabama School of Fine Arts, I knew I needed to find my people again. I wanted to continue my writing career, even while teaching full-time, but I knew to do so, I needed a group of women cheering me on along the way. I needed See Jane Write.

Like so many good things, this story starts with tacos.

On March 24, 2011, I invited a group of women to meet me for dinner at a Mexican cantina near downtown Birmingham. Most of these women I'd never met before; they didn't know me or one another. But we all had one thing in common: we all loved to write.

Some of them were poets who saw writing as music, the song of the soul. Others were fiction writers obsessed with creating imaginary worlds. Some of us were journalists determined to give a voice to the voiceless and share other people's stories. Others were bloggers and essayists, slowly finding the courage to share the stories of their own lives.

I invited these women there that evening for one simple reason: I wanted to start a networking group for women writers. I must admit I wanted to start this group for selfish reasons. I wasn't setting out to change lives. I started the group because I was lonely.

While I was quite fond of my new teacher friends, I missed the group of women writers I was surrounded by in my newsroom. I searched for a women's writing group that would welcome poets, authors, journalists, and bloggers—all hats I'd worn at one point in my writing life—but couldn't find one. So, I decided to start an organization of my own.

I found the women who met me for dinner that evening by becoming a bit of a stalker. I browsed the Internet for Birmingham–based bloggers and scanned the mastheads of local magazines and the bylines in local papers. I checked library listings for readings by local authors. I sent dozens of emails and so many Facebook messages that my account was temporarily suspended until I could prove I was human and not a robot sending out spam.

On March 24, 2011, about a dozen women showed up, and I was elated. This would be the first official gathering of an organization now known as See Jane Write. Over tacos and queso, we discussed our current writing projects and what we would want from a women's writing group. During our conversation, one woman brought up Twitter and how useful it could be for writers. Most of the women at the table weren't buying it. They thought Twitter was stupid. Then one woman turned to me and asked, "Could a workshop on Twitter be our next event?" I thought to myself, *Oh crap! They want another event*! I hadn't actually thought that far ahead. But I made it happen.

I hosted a workshop on Twitter's usefulness for writers for the next event. Forty women attended this event. Next, I hosted a panel discussion on blogging, and seventy-five women showed up.

Today See Jane Write is an award-winning website and business with dues-paying members and an online community of women from cities across the country and worldwide. For See Jane Write, I host monthly events, including workshops, writing critique sessions, and networking mixers. In addition, I produce informative content meant to help women with writing, blogging, and personal brand building, and I offer coaching and consulting programs.

I started See Jane Write for myself. But I've continued it all these years—while juggling a full-time teaching job most of that time—for the women who are part of this group. I continue See Jane Write for members like the plus-size style blogger who in 2016 self-published a book on how blogging about fashion and fitness helped her learn to love her body. I continue See Jane Write because through it, I have helped a woman who always dreamt of being a columnist but never thought she could because she didn't have a journalism degree, see her byline on the front page of local newspapers and on the masthead of local magazines. I continue See Jane Write because members have earned book deals and national speaking engagements, landed full-time jobs because of their blogs, and turned their blogs into profitable businesses.

But most of all, I continue See Jane Write for the members who have found the courage to write about difficult topics like coping with the suicide of a loved one, healing from sexual assault, or surviving domestic abuse. The women of

See Jane Write have found the strength to write themselves back together again. They are becoming the authors of their own lives.

A friend of mine calls See Jane Write, "the sisterhood of the traveling pens." When I was diagnosed with breast cancer, I found out that the women of See Jane Write were my sisters indeed. My sisters were my prayer warriors and did everything in their power to remind me that I'm a warrior too. They sent me T-shirts with slogans like "Faith Over Fear" and "#seejavaciabeatcancer." They bought blankets to help keep me warm in the cold chemo room. And when the chemo took my hair, they sent headscarves. They sent me ginger chews to help me fight nausea and gift cards to my favorite stores just to brighten my day. In my email and social media inboxes, I found affirmations, scriptures, and links to inspirational songs. And the list goes on and on.

A lot of great things have happened to me because of See Jane Write. *Birmingham Business Journal* recognized me as one of the city's Top Forty under Forty. *Southern Living* magazine featured me on its list of Innovators Changing the South, a list that included household names like Dolly Parton and actress Reese Witherspoon. *Black Southern Belle* included me on its list of top tastemakers of the South. See Jane Write helped me land my own magazine column—twice—and allowed me to build a brand and enough buzz for myself that I eventually was able to become my own boss. But all of the awards, accolades, and opportunities pale in comparison to the love and light these women showed me during the darkest time of my life.

Don't try to go through this writing world alone. In her book *Writing Down the Bones*, Natalie Goldberg says that writing is a communal act. She urges you to "write with the whole world in your arms."[1] With See Jane Write, I am doing precisely that.

Writing Prompts:

When you were growing up, what made you different from your peers?
Write about how you have cultivated community or how you've gotten by without it.
Write about a childhood experience that has helped shape who you are today.

Something Like a Love Poem

I was seven or eight years old when I wrote my first poem. My best friend at the time was about to move away, and I was angry with him for being willing to leave me as if a seven or eight-year-old had control over where he lived. But I was angry, nonetheless. And when I get angry, especially irrationally so, I get mean. I figured his departure would be easier to handle, the lump in my throat easier to melt if I pushed him away first. But as soon as the moving truck pulled away, I realized how foolish I'd been.

I wrote him a poem to apologize. The poem was terrible, of course, and I'm pretty sure it contained the line "Roses are red, violets are blue." But this poem began a lifelong love affair—not with the boy who was moving away, but with the written word. It was with that really bad poem that I fell in love with writing.

My bad poetry got a bit better in high school as adolescent angst and teenage crushes fueled my verse. In college as a journalism major and creative writing minor, I flirted with nearly every genre of writing just as I flirted with nearly every type of boy—pretty boys who made me feel ugly, artsy boys who made me feel shallow, religious boys who made me feel dirty, and, of course, bad boys who broke my heart. But heartbreak is good for the poet's pen, I told myself.

Until I met Edward.

Writing brought us together. I met Edward in the summer of 2002 at *The Courier-Journal* in Louisville, where I was an intern, and he was a copy editor. Yes, he was dating the intern, but it wasn't as scandalous as it sounds. Hired immediately after college, Edward was only two years older than we interns were and younger than everyone else on the copy desk by at least two decades. At first, we were just friends, bonding over music, writing, and our mutual love of fruit snacks and gummy bears.

But I still had another semester of college to complete at the University of Alabama that fall and an internship to work at *Health* magazine in Birmingham in the spring. And during this time, I still had a thing for boys who weren't worth my time. Meanwhile, Edward sent me care packages on holidays and flowers "just because."

I returned to Louisville in the summer of 2003 for an internship with the Associated Press. I returned to Louisville for Edward. That summer, Edward and I finally affixed a label to our relationship. I can't say that Edward was the man of my dreams because he surpassed anything I could invent. I could have never imagined this man who would tell me I was beautiful when I was wearing no makeup and my hair was in a messy bun; this man who loved God and made me feel my body was sacred and holy; this man whose conversations somehow made me fall in love with him and with myself.

But can I be a good writer if I'm happy? I actually asked myself this question after Edward and I got serious because there was no more heartbreak to pour into poetry or prose. But that changed once my pursuit of a master's degree put 3,000 miles between us. In August 2003, I moved to Berkeley, California, for a two-year graduate journalism program at the University of California, Berkeley. Just as writing brought Edward and me together, it was now threatening to tear us apart.

You could say I was homesick my first semester at Berkeley, but only if you mean it literally. I had stomachaches, migraines, panic attacks, and trouble catching my breath. And there was the crying. I started crying at the Birmingham airport the day I left for California, and for months it seemed the tears just wouldn't stop. I cried in the morning while brushing my teeth. I cried in the shower while washing my hair. I cried walking to and from classes each day, and I cried myself to sleep each night. I missed my family. I missed my friends. I missed Edward.

Though I made several great friends at Berkeley, friends that I still keep in touch with today through social media, the journalism department had its fair share of elitist, condescending white people who, if they didn't think it beneath themselves to believe in God, would have sworn on a stack of Bibles that they were progressive, empathetic, and (as some say today) woke. I felt inadequate and alone, and each day I thought about dropping out.

But then poetry saved me.

During my second semester at Berkeley, I took a class in the African American Studies department called Poetry for the People. Started by the late renowned poet June Jordan, Poetry for the People was so much more than a class. It was an academic program that exposed students to the poetry of marginalized groups and empowered us to write poetry of our own.

Students could eventually become teachers too. After taking the Poetry for the People course, you could then apply to take another class that would teach you how to lead one of the Poetry for the People classes. I would eventually become a student instructor for Poetry for the People. Through Poetry for the People, I studied and taught African American poetry, Native American poetry, Asian American poetry, Arab American poetry, and works by writers of the LGBTQ+ community. Through P4P (our nickname for the program), I had the chance to read my poetry at venues across the Bay Area and taught writing workshops not just at Berkeley but at community centers and high schools in Oakland. I figured out at an early age that through writing, I could empower myself, but P4P showed me that by teaching writing, I could empower other people too. It was through this program that I found a purpose and my people.

I also found my voice, the voice that I had somehow lost, the voice that had slipped out my back pocket or perhaps fallen from a hole in my bag as I walked the halls of the school of journalism. During P4P, I wrote poetry about politics, race, religion, and even how belittled I felt in most of my journalism classes.

***

In the Graduate School of Journalism

We sit around large wooden tables
In small white rooms
Rattle off resumes and revered readings in
Harpers
New Yorker
Atlantic Monthly

But my momma and Mother Jones ain't never met
And maybe my voice too brown
For Vanity Fair
Maybe my Southern accent
Everyone here calls sweet
Like it's a cupcake
Slice of apple pie
Is really too tart for the taste buds of Berkeley's elite

And where I'm from, eviction notices
Not the New York Times
Were delivered to our doors

So graduate school becomes a study of my inadequacy

I hate the sound of my own words
Click of my own thoughts
In-class comments caught in my throat
Halted by internal instructions
Diagram sentence
Check subject-verb agreement
Yank back the y'alls
Don't let slang slip

I want to scream out
No
I cannot appreciate your use of the word
Negro
In a story about the South
No
I am not soaked with sympathy for white reporters
Who risk being "the other"
Gallop through the ghetto
Descend on Africa

But I just fall in line

Boast about my reporting gig
With the Associated Press
Lie and say I never miss
An issue of the Columbia Journalism Review

And as I reach for worthiness
In this ritual revolving around
This large wooden table
In this small white room
My tiny Black voice
Is cast aside
Like yesterday's news.

***

I wrote a poem about the first boy I ever wrote a poem about!

Honeysuckle

Mama announces summer with a pair of scissors
Clipping the legs from my jeans
Bound to be high waters by fall

We search alleyways
We know we're not supposed to be in
Looking for first, second, and third base
That big oil spot right there will be home
And Keon always brings the ball

My kicks send that red orb
Wobbling across the pavement of the parking lot
Sounding like Daddy's Anita Baker record
That's too worn to play his favorite songs
But you pick me for your team anyway
Every game
And you're the only boy I let kiss me
When we play hide and go seek

We fling off our shoes
Race to the bushes growing along the fence
That's supposed to keep out crime
See how much honeysuckle we can pick
Before the fireflies come out to show off

Our sweaty brown skin glowing in the sunset
As we return home to greet our mamas
With sticky hands and dirty feet

***

And, of course, I wrote poetry about Edward.

Best Poem I Never Wrote

Can metaphor describe
Those rose petals you call fingertips
That river you call a tongue

Can vertical rhythm rock
To the boom of the bass
You bounce to

Can a line break-
Down
Scripture
Teach Jesus to teenagers

Does anything rhyme with copy editor?

Is end rhyme ripe enough for me
To say you have the patience of a tree
Or ask How dare hyperbole
Accuse your simile
Of not really
Clearing cloudy days

Will I lack clarity
Trip into cliché
If I say
I climbed into your eyes
And saw myself for the first time

Perhaps

But when you strut into the room
Spoken words hush
Slam poets concede and take time to breathe
For any poet would know
You're the best poem I never wrote

Through hourly texts, nightly phone calls, and quarterly visits, our long-distance love survived. Then, in May 2005, I graduated from Berkeley and moved back to Louisville to work as a reporter for *The Courier-Journal.* Less than a year later, in April of 2006, Edward and I became husband and wife.

In 2009 we moved to my hometown of Birmingham when I decided I wanted to leave my life as a full-time journalist for a career in teaching. In Birmingham and beyond, Edward and I are seen as an aspirational couple or #relationshipgoals. However, I can tell you that for us, life ain't been no crystal stair.

Our first year of marriage was particularly tough, and I can admit that it was all my fault. My fiercely independent state of mind couldn't quite grasp the idea of "two become one." I wanted separate bank accounts, separate grocery lists, and even separate laundry baskets. Fed up, one day, Edward turned to me and said, "Javacia, I'm your husband, not your roommate!"

Thinking back on these days, I once wrote a letter to my single self that was published in *B-Metro*, a Birmingham–based magazine for which I wrote a monthly column.

Letter to My Single Self

Dear Miss Javacia Nicole Harris,

Congratulations on your engagement. I know you're starting to stress out already, wondering how you're going to plan a wedding in five months with little help and little money. But remember that your wedding is just one day. It's what you do after April 8, 2006, that matters most.

Your first year of marriage will be tough. Your fierce independence will make it quite difficult for you to share everything from a bank account to a bathroom with another person. There will be moments when you'll ask yourself if you can be a feminist and a wife. You can.

You can be a feminist wife because you are also a woman of faith. Pray a lot. After one year of marriage—after one year of struggling with the idea of "two becoming one"—you will pray for a more selfless heart, and everything will change.

You can be a feminist wife because you are marrying a man who sees you as nothing less than his equal, and he will treat you as such. He will be your biggest supporter as you boldly go after your dreams. Be sure that you're his biggest cheerleader as he pursues his goals too.

You're marrying a man who believes in an egalitarian marriage as much as you do, a man who believes housework should be teamwork. There will be no assumption that because you have two X chromosomes, you are required to handle all the housework on your own. You may do most of the cooking, but he will do most of the laundry. He will clean the bathrooms while you clean the other rooms of your apartment. You will buy groceries; he will balance the checkbook. And you will take turns doing the dishes. When your friends say that your husband is a great guy for helping out around the house, he'll be confused. He'll say, "Why shouldn't I help out? I live here too."

That comment will make you fall in love with him all over again.

Remember that you fell in love with him in the first place because he is your best friend. Don't forget to have fun. Laugh at movies. Stay up all night talking and eating junk food. Go for a run together the next morning to burn it off. Tell him your secrets. Tell him your hopes and fears. Tell him when you're hurt or angry, even if he's the one who hurt you or made you mad.

And when he does make you angry, remember he is your family. You and your husband are a family even if you never have children. You will create traditions and great memories and have unconditional love for each other, and that's what family is all about. Chances are, your marriage will last longer if you see your husband as your family the moment you say, "I do." People often remain dedicated to their family members despite mistakes and imperfections. Do the same for your spouse. He's your family too.

Be your husband's girlfriend. When you go out to dinner, get dressed up like it's your first date. Wear cute underwear. Paint your toes. Don't let romance be replaced by the mundane. Don't get so caught up in your daily to-do lists that you forget to make him feel special. He won't. He will send you flowers just because and send you text messages in the middle of the day to tell you that you're beautiful.

One day you won't agree. One day, sooner than you think, you'll look in the mirror, you'll step on the scale, and you won't like what you see. Your husband will wish you could see yourself as he sees you, but he'll understand that won't be enough. He'll give you the time to restore your confidence on your own. He'll give you the space to rediscover who you really are.

Eventually, you will decide to take your husband's last name even though currently, the feminist in you doubts you ever will. Don't view this as defeat. See it as symbolism. See it as the mark of a new era of your life, just as characters in the Bible often had their names changed after a spiritual transformation.

When you decide to call yourself Javacia Harris Bowser, it will signify what you have finally learned: You can be both your husband's wife and yourself. This is what being a feminist wife is all about.

Love,
Mrs. Javacia Harris Bowser

***

Throughout our marriage, my husband and I have lived very busy lives—especially when I was juggling being a teacher, writer, and entrepreneur while he juggled his job as deputy director of communications for the mayor of Birmingham, his work leading the youth ministry at his church, and his efforts to grow and maintain his own personal brand and blog. To spend time with each other outside of our bedroom, we have to sit down with a calendar each month and actually schedule quality time. Whenever I feel this quality time is a bigger priority to me than to him, I find myself acting like an eight-year-old again, pushing him away at the first sign that he may not love me as much as I love him. I pray I don't find myself once again watching a moving truck drive away, realizing what a fool I've been.

I don't write poetry much anymore, so I have no verse with which to compose a lyrical apology. But I still turn to words. Sometimes an email filled with fragments. Sometimes a handwritten note filled with scripture:

> *Where you go, I will go, and where you stay, I will stay. Your people will be my people and your God my God. Where you die, I will die, and there I will be buried. May the Lord deal with me, be it ever so severely, if even death separates you and me.*
>
> *—Ruth 1:16-17*

Sometimes I dig up poems from the past to read to him and remind him that I love him even when I'm being too childish to show it.

Childhood Crush

As I remember the days
Of whipping through the thick blanket
Of Alabama's summer air
My no-name brand sneakers
Racing me to the candy lady
Before she takes her nap
I wish you had been there

We'd put our change together
Buy two cherry bee-bops
(I think in Virginia
Y'all called them frozen cups)
A bag of fruit chews
And a big pickle we'd split in half
You know the kind
You put in a sandwich bag
To save the juice
Our hands would smell of dill for days
I'd stick my fingers under your nose
You'd tickle my bare dirty feet
Until I promise not to do it again

You told the preacher
Our families
And our God
That you would be my happily ever after
But I want you in my once upon a time

I want you to be my childhood crush
To pull my hair
Slide me a note asking if I'd be your girl
I'd check "Maybe"

I want you there to dare me
To run onto the porch
Of that haunted house
With the bats and broken windows
And to hold my hand
When I decide to do it

I want to be one of the boys
And sit next to you at wrestling matches
To help you cheer on Mr. Perfect

I want you to come to my house
When your Daddy refuses
To turn on the A/C
In the middle of July
Because he's convinced Popsicles
Work just as well

I would give you all
The money from my babysitting job
When that burglar
Steals all your Nintendo games

And you'd hold me
In your scrawny adolescent arms
When my parents fight
About strange phone calls
And empty bottles of gin

And when we fight
We'd remember
How we always
Pushed each other on the swings
And realize that marriage
Really can be
As simple as taking turns

***

Any doubts I had in my mind about how much Edward loved me disappeared when I was diagnosed with breast cancer. To be honest, I was surprised by how fiercely he loved me during my treatment. On a Thursday afternoon in January of 2020, I went in for a mammogram that was only meant to establish a baseline for future tests, and the doctor saw something troubling on the scan and the ultrasound that followed. I came home and told Edward that I had to go back to the doctor for a biopsy and that I might have cancer.

"Don't say the c-word," he replied, his tone dismissive as if I were being overly dramatic. He quickly changed the subject.

The biopsy was scheduled for Tuesday, and I was to come in on Friday to review the results. Those days of waiting were torture, and I felt completely alone because Edward didn't seem to be taking any of this seriously. Later, however, I would learn that he was simply scared. He couldn't bear to talk about me having cancer because he couldn't bear to think about it.

On Friday, January 24, 2020, I was diagnosed with invasive lobular carcinoma. I still remember coming home after getting the news and sitting on the side of the bed, unable to speak. Edward knelt beside me, touched his forehead to mine, and whispered, "My wife has cancer." His heart was shattered. I could hear it in his voice. After my diagnosis, he started having a recurring nightmare about someone breaking into our house and trying to hurt me. It doesn't take a literature professor to get that symbolism.

But he picked up the pieces and put himself back together again to be strong for me. On the day of my lumpectomy, he was by my side holding my hand up until the moment the anesthesia sent me drifting away. After leaving the hospital, I found he had flowers and Double Stuf Golden Oreos—my favorite cookies—waiting for me at home.

During my first follow-up appointment with my surgeon, the doctor noticed a mole on a breast and, to rule out the possibility of this being a sign of more cancer, he asked if it had always been there. "Yes," my husband answered before I could. At that moment, I thought to myself, this man has memorized my skin. He knows my body by heart.

When I started to lose my hair from the chemotherapy, Edward helped me chop off my locks, cutting them down to just a few inches. Instead of shaving my head, I let the rest fall out, bit by bit. Once all my hair was gone, I never let him see my bald head. It wasn't that I was ashamed of it. In fact, I was somewhat fascinated by how different I looked. I'd sometimes stand in the bathroom mirror and just stare at my scalp. But I knew that my bald head would just remind him that cancer was taking so much from me and threatening to take me from him.

My headwraps were *always* intact. One day, without me knowing, Edward took photos of me seated on the sofa watching TV. I was wearing shorts, a T-shirt, and a blue and white headwrap, and Edward declared, "You look so regal."

While I was undergoing chemotherapy, Edward would check on me every half hour, insisted that I not wash a single dish, and often would hold my face in his hands and say, "My wife is very pretty." And when it all felt too much to bear, and I'd just break down and sob, he'd wrap his arms around me to remind me that I didn't have to bear this burden alone. Today, I'm ashamed that I thought he wouldn't be my anchor through this storm. Yet, I shouldn't have been surprised by how supportive Edward was during this nightmare because he's always been just as supportive about my dreams.

I won't say I could have never accomplished my writing and business goals without Edward, but having a supportive partner has made a huge difference. He doesn't mind doing household chores when he sees me busy writing, and he edits my work when I'm done. When I host in-person events for See Jane Write, he's there helping to set up, clean up, and sometimes he's even working the registration table. He promotes my blog posts on his social media accounts, and when I receive accolades for my work, he's by my side at every awards ceremony.

In 2016, I started hosting an event called the See Jane Write Wine Down. It was a gathering at a local wine bar and lounge, a girls' night out of sorts, but one with a distinct purpose. The See Jane Write Wine Down was meant to give female writers, bloggers, and entrepreneurs an opportunity to meet with other women on a similar journey to share their troubles and get encouragement and support.

This all came about because of a conversation I had with a fellow female entrepreneur at a networking event. Just as I was at the time, she was building a business while working a full-time job. She was also a wife and a mother, and her husband was getting restless with the late nights and early mornings she was spending working on her dream.

She wasn't the only woman I knew fighting this battle. At blogging conferences, I would often meet women asking for advice on how to get her spouse or significant other to get on board with her goals. So, one day, I simply asked Edward why he was so supportive of my writerpreneur dreams.

"Part of marriage is realizing that your partner's goals and dreams are also your goals and dreams," he responded. He also said he knows I can't succeed if he doesn't give me the space to do so.

I asked if there was anything that he thought the women I'd been chatting with could do to get their boo on board. He said it's important for us dreamers to make our partners feel included. Share the goals you've set for the year and the plans you've plotted to make those dreams come true.

"Don't just tell everybody on Facebook; tell your partner," Edward said.

I should say this—my husband is a blogger as well. So that makes it a bit easier for him to understand my writing goals. But he's not an entrepreneur and has never had aspirations of being one. Yet, my very cautious and extremely frugal husband is okay with me spending money on my business and taking financial risks. He even encouraged me to take the leap in 2019 to quit my teaching job to write and run my business full time.

"You have to believe in your partner's goal, and part of that means letting go of the pocketbook," he said. "You can't make money if you don't spend it."

Whether going after goals or fighting cancer, Edward and I are partners in the truest sense of the word. We're a team. And that is why he always has my back.

"When you shine," he said, "I shine."

Writing Prompts:

Write a poem for someone you love.
Write a letter to your former self or your future self.

Dear God, I Wish You Were a Woman

Trust in God; She will provide.
—Emmeline Pankhurst

Dear God,
I wish You were a woman
Because since I was a girl
I've pictured you as a white man
With white hair
Dressed in a long white robe.
And I am not a man
And my skin is a shade of deep chocolate brown.
So how can I believe that I was created in Your image?

Dear God,
I wish You were a woman
Because sometimes feminism feels like my religion.
Because conversations with other women fill me with the Holy Ghost
More than any church service ever has.
Because the pro-woman words of my favorite girl-power anthems
Move me more than any hymn ever could.
Feminist: a person who believes in the social, political, and economic equality of the sexes.
This is my Apostles' Creed.

Dear God,
I wish You were a woman so I could stop whispering the words,
"She so loved the world"
And start boldly proclaiming them instead.

Dear God,
Sometimes I believe You are a woman
Sometimes I believe that feminine, yet fierce, yet friendly voice
That I hear in my heart
That I hear in my head
Guiding me, comforting me, cheering me on
That voice that as a child I thought must be the imaginary friend
adults said I should have
That voice that as a woman I thought was proof that I was losing my mind
Sometimes—I believe that voice is You.

I think.
I hope.
I pray.

Jesus Is My Homeboy

Long before the popularity of the Jesus Is My Homeboy T-shirts, I considered Jesus my BFF. More accurately, he was my hero, protecting me from an entity much more terrifying than any imagined monster underneath my bed: God. Though prayer was a priority in my household, my parents didn't go to church much; however, as soon as I showed an interest in religion, my granny made sure I was there most Sundays. After listening to a plethora of sermons and memorizing a heap of Bible verses, one day, I told her, "I like Jesus way more than I like God."

She gasped as if I'd just said a dirty word.

"Don't say that," she snapped. "Jesus is God."

I was now utterly confused.

To me, God was a white man with a white beard wearing a white robe and sitting on a white cloud waiting to strike me down once my bad deeds filled up his white tablet. He made note of each time I took change from my Lenten folder for visits to the candy lady or the ice cream truck. He remembered each time I cursed while listening to rap music.

Jesus, however, was the best friend of my dreams, literally. At night I'd dream of Jesus teaching me how to be better at kickball and taking me back-to-school shopping, buying me clothes my parents could never afford. Sometimes we'd take walks in parks, but not the parks in my neighborhood where drug deals went down as soon as the sun did. We strolled in the nice parks made for rich white folks, parks I'd never go to in my real life because rich white people scared me much more than drug dealers ever did.

Despite this, Jesus, my homeboy, was white. But I didn't mind. His hair was coarse and thick like mine, so he never asked to touch my tresses. His face was not the face of a white man who would wield a billy club on brown bodies. He had a boyish face, a mouth that always seemed to be on the verge of a smile, and eyes that twinkled. I figured my white Jesus would never make fun of me for "talking like a white girl," as I was sure a Black Jesus would.

My granny's declaration that Jesus was God pushed me to read the Bible every single day, eager to figure out if she was right. But the more I learned, the less I understood. The Bible just convinced me that there was no way Jesus could be God. Jesus would never flood the world or burn down a city. Jesus would never ask someone to kill their own son. Jesus would never turn me into a pillar of salt. The Bible showed me that I was right all along. Yes, Jesus was my Savior, saving me not from sin but from the wrath of his terrifying Father.

In middle school, however, I learned that I was, in fact, not saved. Even though I read the Bible every day and hung out with Jesus in my dreams every night, I found out I couldn't call myself a Christian because I had never prayed the prerequisite prayer. I had never invited Jesus into my heart (even though I was sure he was already there), and I had never asked him to be Lord of my life (even though I was sure he already was).

In eighth grade, my boyfriend, a preacher's kid, invited me to one of those Christian haunted houses where you go to different rooms to see scenes of what life will be like on earth for those left behind after the Rapture. After sweating in fake hell, I prayed and asked Jesus to save me from the real one. After this, I *did* feel different. My bones felt full of fire, my heart too big for my chest. I decided this feeling was the Holy Spirit that the old folks at church would shout about. And I knew I was finally saved.

Then I went to high school.

Now attending a special school for students gifted in the arts and sciences, I found myself around the most diverse group of people I had ever experienced. No longer at a predominantly Black inner-city public school, I was around white students, Indian students, Asian students, Middle Eastern students, and Hispanic students. I met people who were Muslim, Hindu, and Buddhist. I even met people who didn't believe in God at all! To make sense of it all, I turned to words.

One day after school, I went to my neighborhood library, checked out books on each of the major world religions, and spent my weekends reading through them all. I even started reading the Book of Mormon and the Quran. Later I would join a program designed to encourage cultural exchange between Black Christian and Jewish teens, through which I learned more about Judaism.

Just as with my study of the Bible, the more I learned, the less I felt I knew. My reading, my searching didn't bring me answers, just more questions. At church, I was being told Christianity was the only true path to God, but suddenly God felt too big to fit into one religion. And how could a person as kind-hearted as Jesus be OK with God condemning people to hell in his name?

In college, my love for Jesus and my love for writing would merge when I started writing my prayers instead of speaking them. I had started going to church with "the white folks," as my family said, and the white folks introduced me to the idea of a prayer journal. I carried my prayer journal with me all the time and would stop to write in it whenever I needed a quick chat with Jesus.

Around this time, I also stopped trying to imagine Jesus as a wrathful God and started imagining God as loving as Jesus. My prayer journal became a collection of love letters to God. My prayers became poetry, and suddenly God was everything and everywhere. God was a post-workout smoothie. God was the sun kissing my brown skin when I would lie on the campus quad reading. Once on New Year's Eve, I felt God with me on the dance floor of a nightclub.

But the more I found God in the world, the less I felt God in church. It was the church telling me my gay friends were sinners. It was the church telling me that my Muslim and Hindu friends were going to hell. And it was the church that first told me I couldn't do something because I was a girl.

For most of my childhood, I was oblivious to gender roles and stereotypes. I climbed trees faster and more fearlessly than the boys in my neighborhood because no one ever suggested that I couldn't—or shouldn't. My mother didn't care if I wore dresses or jeans. My father was the one who cooked Sunday dinner and most other meals too.

But it was the church that taught me girls were to be seen, not heard. It started when I got kicked out of a vacation Bible school class one summer at my cousin's church for asking too many questions about Proverbs 31. When I got older and even more interested in religion, I told my granny I had thought about being a preacher one day, and she told me that would never be allowed because the Baptist church believed the pulpit was no place for a woman. This was long before I called myself a feminist, long before I even really understood what that word meant. Yet, when my well-intentioned grandmother said those words, something stirred within me and gave me a command as clear as God's to Moses through the burning bush: "Rebel!"

I declared myself a feminist when I was in graduate school, and in some ways, it felt like declaring war because from that moment until this one, I've felt my feminist ideals and my Christian beliefs battling inside my heart, my mind, my soul. What are God's correct personal pronouns? Once I became a flaming feminist, it got harder to use the pronouns He/Him/His when writing or talking about God. But I was too much of a coward to boldly declare, "Trust in God; She will provide," like Emmeline Pankhurst. Honestly, even that felt incomplete. Sometimes I did need God to be a Heavenly Father. Other times I needed God to be a Divine Mother, a Soul Sister, or a Rich Auntie.

When I was a high school English teacher, a few of my students were transgender, and some were non-binary, so I added "preferred pronouns" to the student info sheets I passed out on the first day of school. This was years before social media platforms would do the same and long before email signatures would jump on board. Yes, a heterosexual, cisgender, Christian teacher in Alabama was ahead of the curve on personal pronouns.

But I was slow to be this open-minded about my spirituality. If I could understand that gender can be fluid in humans and doesn't have to conform to "male" and "female" alone, why couldn't I understand that this could be true of God as well? After all, I did believe we were all created in God's image. So couldn't God be male, female, and everything in between?

I thought this would all be a lot easier if I were a Jesus feminist. Sarah Bessey, the woman who coined the term, defines a Jesus feminist as a person who is a feminist because of her (or his) commitment to Jesus. "Jesus made a feminist out of me," Bessey declared in her 2013 book *Jesus Feminist.* I am not a Jesus feminist. I cannot say that I am a feminist because of my Christianity because, most days, I feel I am a feminist despite my religious beliefs.[1]

I am an intersectional feminist; a feminist who believes issues of race, class, and sexual orientation intersect with issues of gender; and a feminist who can't sit comfortably in the pews of churches that stay silent about police brutality, churches that shun the gay, lesbian and transgender community, or churches that don't open their doors and their hands to the poor. Sometimes I stop going to church altogether. There was a time when I became so disillusioned with the church that I stopped calling myself a Christian. I didn't want to be associated with the sexism, racism, xenophobia, and homophobia that I had started associating with the Christian church. So I stopped saying I was a Christian and started saying, "Jesus is my spiritual guru." But soon, I realized this was no different than people who say they believe in the equality of the sexes but swear they aren't feminists.

Once during one of my church sabbaticals, as I like to call them, my husband, a man of unwavering faith, said to me, "You don't let anyone define your feminism. So why do you let racist, sexist, and homophobic so-called Christians dictate your faith?"

It was a great question, and I knew the answer.

Whenever someone tries to challenge my feminism because they believe feminism is about hating men or that feminism is only for white women, I simply hold fast to the dictionary definition of the word. I am a feminist because I believe in the social, political, and economic equality of the sexes. No one can do or say anything to make me not believe in the equality of the sexes, and therefore no one can do or say anything to make me not call myself a feminist. Even when people who call themselves feminists do or say things I don't agree with, I don't let their words or actions define my feminism. I believe I am free to live out my feminism in any way I see fit as long as I am true to the primary intention of the movement.

I need a simple statement of faith that I can cling to as I do this dictionary definition of feminism. But there is nothing simple about religion. In the New Testament, someone asks Jesus, "Teacher, which is the greatest commandment in the Law?" Jesus answers, "'Love the Lord your God with all your heart and with all your soul and with all your mind.' This is the first and greatest commandment. And the second is like it: 'Love your neighbor as yourself.' All the Law and the Prophets hang on these two commandments."[2]

I wish someone in the crowd would have asked follow-up questions because as I try to cling to this as the foundation of my faith, I need to know how. How do I love God with all my heart, with all my soul, and with all my mind? Perhaps Jesus anticipated this question of mine when he told the disciples, "Truly I tell you, unless you change and become like little children, you will never enter the kingdom of heaven."[3]

Maybe I need to pray like a girl. Maybe I need to go back to carrying my prayer journal with me and writing love letters to God anytime, anyplace. Maybe I need to go back to the days of feeling God everywhere and in everything. Maybe I need to go back to the days of reading the Bible and studying religion not so I could win debates about faith, but simply so I could get to know God.

Maybe I need to go back to the days of meeting Jesus in my dreams. Maybe instead of taking me shopping for back-to-school clothes and going with me to fancy parks, we can go to Black Lives Matter rallies, National Organization for Women meetings, and Pride parades. Maybe I need to go back to church not because I need to do so for God to love me but because at church, I can learn new ways to love God and meet new people to love in God's name.

While feminism is primarily about equality, to me, it's also about sisterhood. I feel this uncanny kinship to nearly every woman and girl on the planet, regardless of race, ethnicity, class, religion, ability, or sexual orientation. This sense of sisterhood drives me to try to empower women and girls in all I do.

Perhaps my love for womankind, for mankind, for humankind—a love that was birthed from my feminism—is exactly what Jesus had in mind when he said, "Love your neighbor as yourself."

While I can't say that I am a feminist because of Christianity, perhaps my feminism will make me a better Christian.

Did God Give Me Cancer?

"God didn't do this, but God will get you through this." That's what one of my friends told me after I was diagnosed with breast cancer in January of 2020. And I wanted to believe her. But I didn't. I was convinced God had given me cancer, and I was pissed.

I started 2020 by going to church every single day. My church was having its annual Twenty-One Days of Prayer. I was fasting sweets, chips, Cheez-Its, and alcohol. That month, I went to church at 6 a.m. every weekday, 9 a.m. every Saturday, and 8 a.m. every Sunday. Each morning I would sit and pray and write in what I call my "Jesus Journal," and I'd never felt closer to God in my life.

Then on day twenty of Twenty-One Days of Prayer, I heard the words, "You have cancer," and I felt betrayed. I was doing all I could think of to be faithful to God, and I was rewarded with this.

Later, after being told for months that my treatment plan would only include surgery and radiation, I found out that chemotherapy might be necessary. My oncologist ran extra tests to be sure. I prayed fervently while waiting for the results, asking God to remove this cup from me.

But that didn't happen.

Prayer became more and more difficult. Asking God for anything felt like a waste of time. I was even afraid to pray, worried that God would give me the exact opposite of what I wanted.

Despite these feelings, I kept going to church–even when God and I weren't on speaking terms. Then the pandemic hit, and the church went virtual. Ironically, it was during this time—when the church was just me, God, and my laptop—that my attitude started to shift. Another friend of mine believed that Twenty-One Days of Prayer was God preparing me for battle, and I began to feel she was right.

I listened to gospel music or sermons while on my daily walks–which kept me grounded during my treatment. I wrote in my prayer journal every day—sometimes twice or even three times a day. I wrote scriptures on pink index cards and carried them with me to chemotherapy. One of the Bible verses I held on to was Genesis 50:20—*"You intended to harm me, but God intended it for good to accomplish what is now being done, the saving of many lives."* I started to believe that something good could come from all the bad.

As spring turned to summer, the senior pastor of my church engaged in some social media activity that made me question where he stands regarding racial injustice. So I stopped logging on for Sunday services. I had planned to find another church to tune in to, but I never did. It just got easy to use that time for something else. Every day I felt myself drifting further and further away from God.

The summer of 2020 was a roller coaster of spiritual highs and lows. One day I'd be praising God that chemo hadn't made me throw up, and then the next day, I'd be angry that I might need a blood transfusion because of low red blood cell counts. Mostly I'd get angry at God when I would think about the aftermath of cancer, when I would think about the fact that my body and my life would never be the same.

But maybe that was the point.

Every December, I choose a word that will be my focus, my theme, for the year to come. My word for 2020 was growth. I was determined that 2020 would be the year I would level up in every aspect of my life. But when you pray for growth, you must be prepared for pruning.

By July, the year 2020 had stripped so much from me–everything from my hair to my hustle. Thanks to cancer, chemo, and COVID-19, my busy schedule—once packed with meetings, lunches, brunches, and networking events–was gone. I would simply wake up, go for my daily walk, work on freelance stories or content for my writing coaching business, watch TV, or read and go to bed. Aside from my walks, I would only leave the house for chemotherapy appointments or to pick up medication from Walgreens. After being so busy for so many years, I should have loved the slow and easy pace. But I hated it.

Eventually, however, I decided to stop throwing temper tantrums in my prayer journal. I decided to stop asking God, "Why is this happening to me?" and started asking, "What is this trying to teach me?"

During active treatment, I rested more than I ever had in my entire life, and yet I made more money as a writer and entrepreneur than I ever had. I learned to work smarter, not harder. And most of all, I learned to let go and let God. As a writer, I've learned that freelancing is an act of faith.

On May 24, 2019, I left my job as a high school English teacher, a job I actually loved, to take a leap into the unknown and begin my journey as a full-time freelance writer. Of course, my biggest fear in taking the leap to work for myself was money. I don't like to say I grew up poor. We always had food to eat and a roof over our heads. But that roof had leaks, that food was often from a can, and I'm no stranger to disconnected utilities or eviction notices.

So once I became a financially secure adult, I had no desire to ever go back.

In January 2020, during Twenty-One Days of Prayer, I came across a verse from the book of Nahum (a book I'm not sure I even knew existed before then) that declares, "trouble will not come a second time." It felt like God was speaking directly to me, letting me know that I would not have to face the money troubles of my childhood ever again. I would find myself repeating this verse, again and again, that year. Before I quit my teaching gig, my husband and I determined how much money I needed to bring in every month for us to pay the bills and maintain our lifestyle. In 2020, I met or exceeded that goal every single month.

Freelancing is an act of faith because it requires that you have faith in God and in yourself. Freelancing also requires faith in your tribe. Relationships I've built over the years with other writers and entrepreneurs paid off–literally. When many of the local publications I write for had to cut their freelance budgets at the height of the pandemic, I still made enough money to pay my bills because I got gigs writing for local businesses and non-profit organizations. I landed lucrative opportunities to write for national media outlets too.

Because of my faith in my God, myself, and my tribe–I was freelancing and doing just fine in 2020. In spite of COVID-19 and cancer, I was not only surviving but thriving. I've learned that sometimes when it seems everything is falling apart, things are actually falling into place.

Did God give me cancer? I have no idea.

***

As I'm writing this, I still haven't found a new church. But in *The Color Purple* Alice Walker writes, "Any God I ever felt in church I brought in with me." And I couldn't agree more.

Don't get me wrong. I believe the church is important for both personal growth and community service. But I don't have to go to church to have a spiritual practice. That's all on me.

When my faith wavers, I turn to words. I believe writing can be a form of worship because it is an act of creation. To have the space, the time, and the freedom to create is a blessing indeed.

I was in college when I first started writing my prayers. And writing has been a part of my spiritual practice ever since. Along with my prayer journal, I keep a journal that's all about my dreams and goals. In it, I write about the things I desire for my life, but I write about them as if they're already my reality. This is a powerful practice! It gets me so excited about the future. And I've noticed that as I'm writing my dreams as if they've already come true, the path for how I will actually achieve them starts to download in my brain.

So one day, I got to thinking, and I wondered if I could use a similar practice to help restore my faith in God. Minister and Christian author Priscilla Shirer says that faith is acting like God is telling the truth. Romans 8:28 says, "And we know that in all things God works for the good of those who love him, who have been called according to his purpose."

I thought, if God is telling the truth, then even cancer, chemo, and anything else I may face will turn into something good for me. I challenged myself to write in my prayer journal as if I had already seen this come to pass. Here's a snippet of one of those prayers:

Thank You for Your faithfulness. Your Word says that You will work out all things for the good of those who love You, and Your Word is true.

Even things as dark as cancer and chemotherapy have been turned around to better my life. I appreciate every person and every little thing in my life in a way I never could before cancer. After conquering cancer, I am confident I can do anything. And all I managed to accomplish while in active treatment is a testimony to Your goodness and Your grace.

I am Job. You have restored everything that chemotherapy took from me. My body is strong, and I take better care of this temple than ever before.

I am Jacob. I wrestled with you until you blessed me. Cancer may have left me with a metaphorical limp, but a woman's walk is supposed to be different after she's been to battle and won.

Writing Prompts:

What do you believe? How have your beliefs changed over time?
How do you define faith? Write about a time you took a leap of faith or faced a crisis of faith.
What do you worship? How do you worship?

I Contain Multitudes

For years I felt as if I were caught in a love triangle—writing and teaching both tugging at my heart. The Ethiopian proverb "She who learns teaches" is one that I live by. I even had it posted in my classroom. But I believe she who writes teaches too.

I was born to teach, but I didn't realize this until after working in education for seven years. When I was a girl, I named all my dolls and other toys, arranged them in nice, neat rows in alphabetical order, and then launched into a lecture on whatever struck my fancy at the time. The classroom called me early in life, though I didn't know it.

But I also was born to write. This I've known since the day I wrote my first poem. I was only seven or eight years old, so it was terrible. But with that poem, I fell in love with writing. And it was this love that led me to study journalism in college.

But a career in education was still whispering in my ear, flirting with my future plans. At UC Berkeley, I was a graduate student instructor, or GSI, and taught a communications class for undergraduate students. I was charged with breaking down the complicated concepts and theories the professor discussed in her lectures. I did such a good job that students assigned to other GSIs would ask to come to my class, willing to sit on the floor or stand in the back if there weren't enough desks.

I applied for Teach for America. I was accepted by Teach for America. I turned down Teach for America. I had also been offered a job as a features reporter in a city that I love with the man I love. Writing won my heart again.

It was during my job as a journalist that I made another important discovery about myself. I wasn't content with simply being a writer. I wanted to be a "feminist writer." I found feminism in a college classroom. Her name was Kate. She was a women's studies major, and I often strained my eye-rolling muscles when she went off on rants about gender inequality — until I started to actually listen to what she had to say and started to wonder if she was right. Then I went to grad school, started learning about the gender gap and the male gaze, and realized that Kate was right—about all of it.

While working in journalism, I was assigned my very own bi-weekly column. I decided to use that platform to confess that I was a true believer in feminism and work out my salvation. My email inbox was flooded with messages from women who proudly identified as feminists too. The owner of a local boutique taped my girl power articles to one of the walls of her store and wrote above them, "We LOVE Javacia."

But the call to teach lingered, telling me I was the one who got away. In 2009, I made the leap, leaving my job as a full-time reporter to teach early American literature (hence the Walt Whitman reference in the title of this essay) at a school for kids gifted in the arts and sciences, a school that also happens to be my alma mater. Being a teacher at this school proved to be just as challenging as being a student there, and suddenly, I felt as if someone had hit the rewind button on my life. I was once again an insecure teenager walking the halls of her high school, wondering what she should do with her life. At least this time, I didn't have acne.

But this time, I also didn't have my squad (or my clique, as we called it in the '90s). I missed being around other women writers. And that's why I started See Jane Write.

Ironically, it was through See Jane Write, not in my classroom, that I realized I was born to teach. I would often say, "I teach like a girl, and I teach grown-up girls too." To teach like a girl meant intersectional feminism was at the core of my curriculum, it meant I will never stop learning, and it meant that I knew I would become the educator I needed to be by remembering the student I used to be. But I would also say I taught "grown-up girls" because my teaching extended far beyond the classroom and into See Jane Write workshops, freelance articles, and blog posts.

See Jane Write, my blog, and my freelance articles became my way to empower women. Writing became my feminist activism.

There was a time when I felt like a fake feminist. Sure, I believe in equality but was I doing something about it? I've never started a petition in support of Planned Parenthood (though I've signed plenty). I didn't do anything to help push the passing of the Lilly Ledbetter Act (though I fan-girled out when I met her in 2016). And I don't even get into intense political debates with my friends on social media. I just write.

But when I wrote about being a feminist wife, I received emails from engaged young women thanking me for showing them they could love their husbands without losing themselves. And at least once a week, I get an email from a See Jane Write member telling me that my organization is helping her finally go after dreams she's been putting off for years.

I've come to believe that writing can be a feminist act. Firstly, through writing, a woman can learn to love herself. I'm speaking from experience. I learned to love my unruly curls by writing articles on African American women and the natural hair movement. I learned to love my dark brown skin by writing about colorism. And I believe self-love is essential for this movement. I think that a woman needs to love herself before she can believe she deserves better than the status quo. But any movement worth its salt must move beyond the empowerment of the individual and work for systemic change. I believe writing can help with this, too, in part by raising awareness. Plus, once a woman loves herself, she's better equipped to do the work needed to transform society into a place where self-love isn't so hard to come by.

Being a feminist writer and being an educator were both rewarding. But eventually, I realized I wanted even more. I wanted to be a boss. Perhaps I've wanted this since my childhood days of selling used goods to family and friends.

In 2019, I quit my teaching job to be what I like to call a full-time "writerpreneur." The decision to leave the classroom was hard, and not just because I knew I'd miss my students and my colleagues. It was hard because I was breaking the rules. I'm a good girl, and I always have been. Just ask my parents or former teachers if you don't believe me. I'm an Enneagram 1, which means I like order. So give me the rules, and I'll follow them–most of the time. (The feminist in me doesn't always follow the rules about what a woman should and shouldn't do or should and shouldn't be–but that's another topic for another essay.)

The rules say you go to college, get a good job, work hard at that job, stack your 401K, and then retire. So I went to college–twice. I got a good job. And then I got another good job. And with each one, I secured a solid salary and benefits–because that's what good girls do.

But then, on May 24, 2019, I did something good girls don't do. I quit! I quit my teaching job to write on my own terms and build See Jane Write, and I made the leap with no safety net beneath me.

Sure, I had a few publications that I wrote for regularly, but that income was just enough to pay for Beyoncé concert tickets, the occasional girls' trip, and Spring Break vacations with my husband. My freelance money was my play money. Now it had to be my mortgage money and my money for everything else!

Was I afraid to jump? Hell yeah, I was scared! I was afraid I wouldn't have enough money to pay my bills or that hubs and I would have to eat peanut butter and jelly sandwiches for dinner every night.

But I jumped anyway. How did this good girl convince herself to break the rules?

One of my favorite quotes states, "You owe it to yourself to become everything you've ever dreamed of being." Through See Jane Write, I get to be all I've ever dreamed of being all at once. Through my blogging and freelancing, I am a writer. Through my online and in-person workshops, I am a teacher. Through building my membership and coaching programs, I am an entrepreneur. And by using all that I do to empower women, I am a feminist at work.

I hope you can see that you can become everything you've ever dreamed of being too.

Cancer Is a Cruel Teacher

I'm a machine.

That's what I would proudly say whenever people would ask me how I do it all.

For nearly ten years, I juggled a full-time job as a high-school English teacher with a freelance writing career and a blog that I turned into a business. I loved the hustle. And I felt I had a good life. Despite my busy schedule, I made time for daily workouts, date nights with my husband, brunch with my girlfriends, and even "Self-Care Saturday."

But most days I was surviving on four to six hours of sleep. Sometimes I'd get so busy I'd forget to eat and then binge once I remembered. *But I can handle it,* I would tell myself. *I'm a machine.*

Then the gears of the machine came screeching to a halt when I was diagnosed with breast cancer. Did I cause this? Did my hustle cost me my health? It's not lost on me that cancer is caused by overactive cells, cells that are doing more than they're supposed to do. Were they just following my lead?

Eight months before my diagnosis, I'd quit my day job. I left the classroom to focus on writing and entrepreneurship. This wasn't an easy decision to make because I loved teaching. But I'd reached my breaking point with "doing it all." As Elaine Welteroth states in her book *More Than Enough*, "There is no glory in a grind that literally grinds you down to dust."[1]

So when I quit my full-time job, I didn't feel that I was choosing between writing and teaching. I was choosing myself.

But maybe I was too late. Was the tumor in my left breast already growing before I handed in my letter of resignation? Was it there as I ate cake at my going away party? Was it there as I sipped margaritas with my girlfriends to celebrate this new chapter in my life? Was it there as I continued to wake up before dawn to squeeze as much work as I could out of each day even after I quit my job?

Cancer put an end to all of that. Chemotherapy left me so exhausted that sometimes I'd sleep for twelve hours. And during active treatment, my workdays were cut down to four hours or less. My high-intensity training workouts were replaced with daily walks through my neighborhood to help clear my mind.

And yet, I never missed a deadline, and in 2020 I made more money than I ever had. By taking on fewer projects that paid more money and being upfront about how much time I needed to complete each one, I was able to work smarter, not harder.

I am not a machine, and I don't need to be. Cancer taught me that.

I am also not the work I do. This was a hard lesson for me. For years, I'd proudly proclaimed, "Writing isn't just what I do; it's who I am." But the trouble with statements like that is we can start to tie our worth to our work. And so, we won't give ourselves a break. We're so caught up with taking care of business that we don't take care of ourselves.

Because of cancer, I now plan all of my meals – making sure I eat enough fruits and vegetables each day. I drink more water and I get more rest. I exercise almost every day – doing workouts I actually enjoy instead of routines that feel like punishment. I take breaks. I say no. Because of cancer I've learned to do the things I should have been doing all along to give my body and myself the love that we deserve.

Cancer is a cruel teacher.

Teach Like a Girl

When I was a teacher, I carried a coffee mug that read "Teacher by day, Blogger by night." By day I taught English to seventh, eighth, and tenth graders. By night I blogged about writing, wellness, and women's empowerment.

But even though my coffee mug declared that I was both a writer and an educator, I worked to keep these two worlds separate. I never talked about my blog at work, and since I often shared my blog posts via social media, I never accepted Facebook friend requests from students. I kept my Twitter account locked so I could control who followed me. But then one day a student came up to my desk and said to me the words I never wanted to hear: "Mrs. Bowser, you know I read your blog."

I wanted to hide under my desk.

I know it was completely irrational for me to believe I could keep something hidden on the internet, but sometimes I am completely irrational. The student went on to say, "From what I've read, I can tell you are a feminist." I should mention that this student was a boy. And I should also mention that even in the twenty-first century, there are still people for whom calling yourself a feminist is akin to dropping the f-bomb at church. I was certain this student of mine was about to ask me if I hated him because he's a boy.

But I was wrong.

Instead, he tucked his mop-like red hair behind his ear and said, "I wanted to ask you … can a boy be a feminist? After reading your blog, I think I might be one."

After that day, I made two decisions: I decided to be very, very careful about what I shared on my blog, but I also decided that I would strive to create a feminist classroom. This may cause complete panic for some people. Some people may imagine me creating some man-hating, Communist mini-cult. Those people would be wrong. And some people who agree with the idea of creating a feminist classroom may imagine I'm telling students how they should feel about abortion and Republicans. And those people would be wrong too.

Creating a feminist classroom, in my opinion, isn't about telling students how they should vote once they're old enough to do so. It's about encouraging them to treat all people with dignity, regardless of gender, race, class, religion, sexual orientation, or ability. A feminist classroom is simply a place that values equality, equity, respect, and representation and makes those values apparent every day.

I believe one of the best ways to cultivate equity and respect in a classroom is by giving students a voice. I gave my students options, and I worked to create a classroom that fostered discovery and discussion and that wasn't solely based on lectures. Sometimes I'd let my students have a say when planning lessons and class activities, and I'd give them the chance to express and work through their thoughts on the various topics we studied and even on current events.

A feminist classroom is also a classroom that values representation. I strove to include commonly marginalized voices in my lesson plans so that my students were learning about writers often excluded from the literary canon. I also encouraged my students to try to examine the topics we studied from different perspectives. Obviously, I tried to develop a variety of activities to speak to different types of learners, but I also worked to acknowledge other facets of my students' lives, such as race, gender, class, ability, and ethnicity. This doesn't mean that I asked students to be the spokesperson for a particular group. But if students wanted to share their individual experiences, I absolutely encouraged that. To create a feminist classroom, I didn't have to wear my Rosie the Riveter T-shirt to class every day, but I wanted to be sure that marginalized voices were represented so that students of all backgrounds left my class with a "We Can Do It" attitude.

When that student asked me if a boy could be a feminist, I told him, "Absolutely!" We talked about how gender stereotypes can be harmful to both boys and girls. And we talked about the negative connotations of the word *feminist*. Then I reminded him that according to that blue dictionary I was always urging them to use when they're reading *The Scarlet Letter* and had no idea what half the words meant, a feminist is simply a person who believes in the social, political, and economic equality of the sexes.

And then he looked at me, smiled, and said, "Yeah, then I'm definitely a feminist. And I'm glad you're one too."

Even after that experience, I still hesitated to mention my writing and blogging life with my students. It's not that I ever wrote anything on any of my websites that I thought would get me fired. It's just that a part of me worried that if my students saw that I was essentially juggling another career it would make them feel I wasn't dedicated to them, that I wasn't serious about teaching.

But I was completely wrong about that. My students loved the fact that I had a thriving writing career in addition to my teaching career. I've had students write on my teacher evaluation forms that knowing that I am a writer made them want to listen to what I told them about essay writing and composition. They said they knew I was telling them that writing is important because I actually believed it, not because I was paid to say so.

I've had students say that reading my writing made them want to improve their own. And I've had students say that the work ethic I had to juggle two careers inspired them to "stop watching Netflix all the time and do something that matters."

After reading enough evaluations like this I realized that being a teacher also meant being a role model. This terrified me. I used to get so annoyed whenever I read or heard about celebrities who said they didn't want to be role models. "You're a role model whether you like it or not!" I'd yell at the TV screen or the magazine in my hands.

But one day I had to declare this to the mirror.

As much as I am irritated with the rich and famous for complaining that young people look up to them, a part of me understands where they're coming from. Being a role model is scary. To know that the words you say and the things you do could have a course-altering effect on a young person's life is petrifying. But it's also inspiring and can be the best motivation for getting out of bed in the morning. By striving to be a good role model you will not only help other people, but you'll also help yourself. Being a role model made me a better person.

Knowing I was a role model to some of my students made me work harder inside and outside the classroom. Obviously, I tried to spark interesting discussions in the classroom and gave students assignments that would make them better writers and thinkers. But I realized the work I did before and after school mattered too. Reading those student feedback surveys showed me that my students were inspired by the fact that I was freelancing for local media outlets and running a women's writing group.

Being a role model can boost your beauty regimen too! The fact that I wear my hair in its naturally curly state inspired many of my African American female students to do the same. And some students even commented on my manicures on class evaluation forms! All this may sound silly, but it's not. If Essie nail polish could help me connect with a student and that connection could help her succeed, then I was willing to apply a fresh coat of polish to my nails every single day if necessary.

As a role model, I had to be mindful of my web presence too. There was a time when only celebrities had to worry about their images in the media, but due to blogging and social media, we all have a public profile to manage. Being a role model meant I had to be mindful of what I was putting out into cyberspace. This doesn't mean being fake. On my blog, for example, I often honestly write about my problems and struggles, but I try not to write about an issue until after I've worked through it or at least learned something from it.

I kept negative self-talk in check too. At school, I never wanted my students—especially my female students—to hear me saying disparaging things about my weight or my looks because I never wanted them repeating those things to themselves. By being a role model, I could have a bigger impact on a student's life than Beyoncé. Seriously!

One day, during a class discussion of celebrities who have publicly embraced feminism, Beyoncé came up. After we all gushed over her awesomeness for about ten minutes, one student said that Beyoncé actually didn't help her embrace feminism—I did. She said that Beyoncé made her interested in feminism but because Beyoncé is, well, *Beyoncé*, she still didn't quite understand how feminism could apply to her everyday life. But after taking my Women and the Media class–an elective I created to teach students how to examine representations of women in the media—she started viewing me as a feminist role model. One who was more relatable than a famous billionaire entertainer.

There's a snarky quote that was once floating around the internet that reads: "Always be yourself, unless you can be Beyoncé. Then always be Beyoncé." But by being a role model I've realized why we should always be ourselves, and our best selves, no matter what.

Chocolate Girl

"Mrs. Bowser, am I chocolate or caramel?" a student once asked me as I was headed to my classroom on what had otherwise been an ordinary day.

"What?" I was confused.

The bell would ring soon signifying the start of class. With no time to waste, she turned to a classmate.

"Hey! Am I chocolate or caramel?" she asked another student making his way down the hall.

"Caramel," he answered.

Apparently, this was the right answer.

"Yes!" the beautiful, brown-skinned girl said in celebration.

She and another Black female student had been arguing with each other over whether they were the color of caramel or chocolate. They even began to poll passers-by in the hallway. They counted each vote for "caramel" as a win.

My heart broke. I thought colorism had gone out of style with Gen Z. I thought things were improving. I was seeing more dark-skinned women on television, in movies, and in magazines. But those instances were still rare enough that they remained a pleasant surprise. Some of my Black female students would sport T-shirts celebrating their skin color, T-shirts that boasted proud slogans like, "That Melanin Though." Yet, I still heard others lamenting their summer tans.

I looked at this girl and wondered if she, like me, had been told she was "pretty for a dark-skinned girl."

Many years before, in the summer of 2003, I was a bridesmaid in the wedding of a longtime friend. At the reception, the mother of another childhood friend, whom I hadn't seen in over a decade, saw my name on the program and decided to search the banquet hall for me to say hello. When she finally found me, she said, "People kept pointing to you saying, 'That's Javacia,' but I didn't believe them. You've gotten so dark. But don't worry, you're still pretty."

This wasn't the first time I'd been told this, and it certainly wouldn't be the last. Nonetheless, this is a statement I'll never get used to. With colorism–discrimination based on skin color–lighter-skinned people are usually favored, sometimes considered smarter, kinder, and more attractive. Colorism is not solely an American issue, as it is a problem in Africa, Southeast Asia, East Asia, India, and Latin America as well. Colorism can exist between different races or within the same race, which is, unfortunately, how I have experienced it most.

As a child, I didn't know the word colorism. But when I overheard one of my uncles jokingly say that if his children had been born dark-skinned, he would have smothered them in the hospital, I did know this so-called joke wasn't funny. When I was a child, my skin tone was much lighter than it is today. But just as a Caucasian child's hair color might change as he or she gets older, so might the skin tone of a person of color. This is common. As I grew older, I grew darker, and I didn't think twice about this until people started to offer me unsolicited comfort, assuring me that I was "still pretty" in spite of my dark brown skin.

Black men flirting with me would often say they'd never met a dark-skinned woman as pretty as I, actually thinking that I would consider that a compliment. And an ex-boyfriend, trying to explain such comments, once told me that light-skinned Black women are more attractive because they're seen as more feminine.

As I looked at my student, I wondered if she, like me, had been told to stay out of the sun. When I, as a grown-ass woman, started signing up for half-marathons, some of my family members told me I needed to stop. Running outside in the sun was only making me darker, they'd say.

I looked at my student's cute, curly coif, and I wondered if she, like me, had been told she had "good hair" and if this phrase made her cringe or if she clung to it like a badge of honor. When I started wearing my hair in its naturally curly state, people would look at the soft ringlets flowing down my back and ask how a dark-skinned person could have such "good hair." It didn't seem right, they'd say.

Years later when I was a bridesmaid for yet another wedding–maybe I need to just stop being in weddings–the bride's hairstylist, who was a very light-skinned Black woman, and turned to me and asked: "How you get hair like that as dark as you are?! I'm damn-near white and my hair don't look like that!"

I know that the roots of colorism and even notions of "good hair" can be traced to white supremacy. And this is why I can forgive friends, family, and even strangers for these comments. But that knowledge doesn't make the words any less hurtful.

That day in the hallway, I wanted to convince my students that chocolate skin is just as beautiful as caramel, but I knew nothing I could say could erase the experiences that had made them think otherwise.

"What's wrong with being chocolate?" I asked.

She looked at me and answered, "Nothing and everything."

And I knew exactly what she meant.

I have come to believe that self-love is a revolutionary act. Whether a person is disparaged because of race, skin color, gender, religion, sexual orientation, or body type, when marginalized people love themselves in spite of society telling them they should not, they are true rebels indeed. And this self-love can often be the first step toward systemic change or cultural shifts.

African Americans in the South loved themselves enough to know they deserved better than what "separate but equal" dogma would allow them. Through the civil rights movement of the 1960s, they dismantled the laws of Jim Crow.

I, too, wish to practice this transformative love—I will love myself enough to know that my skin color is not a flaw. And my hope is that my confidence will be contagious to the teen girls in my life. I will love myself enough to run freely in the sun, with my curls dancing in the wind.

Writing Prompts:

What's the best advice you have to give? Tell the story of how you learned this life lesson.
Tell a story of a mentor or teacher who helped shape your worldview or guided you through a challenging time.
Have others ever made you feel insecure about your physical appearance? How did you learn to love yourself in spite of this?

How I Stopped Worrying and Learned to Love My Name

Let's be frank, my name is REALLY, REALLY BLACK. If you saw my name listed somewhere, you'd know I'm a Black chick even if my picture weren't beside it. Growing up, people told me my name was a liability. They told me that because my namc is SO BLACK, I often would be passed over by certain employers.

As a girl, while my friends were thinking of names for their future kids, I would sit in my room jotting down ideas for the pseudonym I would use when I became a published writer. I was disrespectful of my name, calling it "ghetto." When people had trouble pronouncing my name I apologized as if I, and the syllables it took to address me, had somehow offended them. When I told people my name and they said, "Well, that's different," I felt ashamed. And when they turned to me with a furrowed brow and asked, "Do you have a nickname?" I just laughed and said, "Yeah. You can call me J."

Perhaps I was so insecure about my name because I've spent over half my life often being the only Black person in the room—in some of my high school classes, in many of my undergrad and graduate school classes, and in my professional life as a journalist and educator. Being the only Black person in the room has meant fielding questions that often begin with the statement "Javacia, why do Black people…" It's meant constantly being asked, "Can I touch your hair?" It's meant dealing with older white men who jokingly referred to me as their "brown sugar girlfriend" while I was trying to conduct interviews.

On top of all this, I have also often found myself surrounded by people from wealthy families—people who never had to figure out how to keep warm in winter when the gas bill couldn't be paid; people who have never come home from school to find an eviction notice taped to the front door. It's because of my family's money woes that I never thought I'd be a homeowner. But on May 14, 2015, my husband and I bought our first house. Moving day felt like Christmas—or what Christmas must have felt like for kids whose families had money.

That morning when the movers arrived to load up our furniture, I ran down the stairs of our apartment building to greet the two men with the truck. I stuck out my hand to one of the movers and said, "Hi. My name is Javacia."

And he laughed.

"What's so funny?" I asked.

"Your name," he replied and continued to giggle.

The look on my face quickly wiped the grin off his. This man, whose skin was the same shade of brown as mine, reminded me that sharing dark skin doesn't always make two people kin. But the Javacia greeting that mover was different. This was not the Javacia who once apologized for her name or wished to change it. This was a new Javacia who knew her name was poetry.

This was the Javacia who is a writer.

When I became a journalist, I fell in love with my byline. The "ghetto" name Javacia proudly made its way into the pages of *The Seattle Times*, *The Chicago Sun*, *USA Today*, and half a dozen national magazines.

When I learned to love my name, I also learned to love the girl who carries it.

I learned to love my curly tresses by writing articles on Black women and the natural hair movement. I learned to love my dark skin by writing about colorism. I learned to be proud of the neighborhoods I grew up in by writing about how growing up with little taught me a lot. It all began with writing, with telling my stories and helping other people share theirs too.

Now I'm on a mission to share this good news, spreading it as if it were the gospel because indeed God did use writing to save me from self-hate and self-doubt. And so See Jane Write is not simply a business; it is a ministry. The networking events I host are communion. The blog posts I publish are virtual evangelical tracts. When the women of See Jane Write and I write together – whether in person or on a Zoom call – the fellowship feels sacred. The informative workshops that I lead I take as seriously as a sermon. The word I have is this: Every woman has a story worth sharing and the power to write her way back to herself.

Writing Prompts:

What is the story of your name?
I was given my name because . . .
I like/dislike my name because . . .
My name is/isn't a good fit for my personality because . . .
Describe a time when someone made an assumption about you because of your name.

Ain't I a Feminist?

It was a simple email–just eight words and no signature. It read: "A black woman cannot be a feminist. Sorry."

I replied, "Why not?"

No answer.

I took it to the tweets and told my Twitter followers what happened. They responded in shock and horror, and they all assumed the author of the email was white. I did not.

Just days before I received the aforementioned email, I had written a guest post for a popular natural hair blog about how embracing my naturally curly coif made me a better feminist. Several commenters on that post couldn't believe I, being a Black woman, would call myself a feminist. Their response reminded me of when I wrote and published a piece for a newspaper in Louisville declaring myself a feminist in print for the first time. My email inbox was flooded with supportive messages from like-minded women. But I also received a message from a Black man who didn't understand why a Black woman would dare associate herself with a movement that was spearheaded by "racist, wealthy white women."

I am not naïve about feminism's history. First-wave feminists and women's suffrage activists, despite being part of the movement to abolish slavery, were infuriated when Black men were given the right to vote before white women. In 1869, during a meeting of the American Equal Rights Association, Elizabeth Cady Stanton stated that "Sambo" wasn't ready for the vote. In an effort to gain the support of white Southerners, Susan B. Anthony forged alliances with groups that opposed voting rights for African Americans and women's groups that excluded Black women.[1] When women gathered in Washington in 1913 for the historic women's suffrage parade, Black women were discouraged from attending or asked to march in the back.[2] And many second-wave feminists of the 1960s and 70s often focused solely on the issues faced by straight, upper-middle-class white women, ignoring the struggles of women of color, poor women, and lesbians.

This problem has continued into the twenty-first century as many white feminists fail to recognize racially motivated police violence as a feminist issue.

And as a proud member of the BeyHive, I'd be remiss to not point out that many of the same white female culture critics who hailed Madonna for her brazen sexuality, accused Beyoncé of mindlessly playing into the male gaze as she began to rise to superstardom.[3]

I am well accustomed to the balancing act of loving something with a sordid past. I was, after all, born and raised in Birmingham. This is a city whose history is colored by the killing of four little Black girls in the bombing of Sixteenth Street Baptist Church, images of high-power water hoses being turned on brown bodies protesting for their civil rights, and tales of the terrors caused by the Ku Klux Klan.

But my city is not a bomb. My city is not a burning cross. My city is my home, and my home has and will continue to raise up artists and activists–of all races and backgrounds—who have and who will continue to transform the South. Likewise, I believe the feminist movement has and will continue to raise up artists and activists—of all races and backgrounds—who have and will continue to transform this country and change this world.

Furthermore, to consider feminism a white woman's movement is to discount all the work that women of color have done in the fight for equality. Case in point, shortly after the #MeToo movement began to make headlines, I found myself at a dinner party discussing Tarana Burke, the founder of the movement, and the contributions of other Black women who were sparking social change. A white woman at the table then asked me why I thought Black women were finally starting to get politically active. I was so shocked by her ignorance I was speechless for a moment.

Then I simply said, "This is not new. Black women have always been in this fight."

Black women were there for the suffrage movement. Sojourner Truth spoke boldly on the issue of women's suffrage stating that if Black men got rights and Black women didn't, "the colored men will be masters over the women, and it will be just as bad as it was before."[4]

As some white suffragists and their organizations refused to include issues of race in their campaigns, Black women began forming groups of their own, groups like the National Association of Colored Women, founded in 1896.[2] The group's first president and co-founder Mary Church Terrell toured the country lecturing on women's voting rights. She spoke out about the hypocrisy of white suffragists who fought for women's rights yet ignored the injustices endured by Black people.[5] Frances E.W. Harper, a founding member of the American Woman Suffrage Association, spoke at the Women's Convention of 1866 and called out white suffragist organizations for racial discrimination.[5]

Nannie Helen Burroughs helped found the Women's Auxiliary of the National Baptist Convention, an organization of more than one million women that she led in support of women's suffrage.[5] Journalist and activist Ida B. Wells worked with white suffragists in Illinois but also founded the Alpha Suffrage Club for Black women. Wells also participated in the 1913 women's suffrage parade and refused to march in the back.[2]

And after the Nineteenth Amendment was passed, Black suffragists continued the fight. For decades after the ratification of the Nineteenth Amendment, women (and men) of color would continue to be disenfranchised, especially in the South. The threat of lynching and other intimidation tactics kept Black men and women from casting their ballots, as did poll taxes, literacy tests, and grandfather clauses. It wasn't until the Voting Rights Act of 1965 that measures designed to disenfranchise racial minorities were outlawed.

Mary McLeod Bethune founded many organizations, led voter registration drives – while facing threats from the Ku Klux Klan – and even worked with presidents of the United States in support of rights for Black women and men.[6] Fannie Lou Hamer – co-founder of the Mississippi Freedom Democratic Party and the National Women's Political Caucus – was vital in the fight for Black women to vote in Mississippi and throughout the South.[7]

Gloria Steinem, who's considered the face of the women's movement of the 1960s and 1970s, has said in several interviews that Black women have always been on the front lines of feminism.[8] Steinem's own feminist activism was shaped by Black women like Flo Kennedy. Kennedy was a civil rights lawyer who was Steinem's speaking partner for years. Dorothy Pitman Hughes co-founded Ms. Magazine and the Women's Action Alliance with Steinem.[9]

Aileen Hernandez was co-founder and the second president of the National Organization for Women. And after leaving NOW, she co-founded the National Women's Political Caucus, Black Women Stirring the Waters, and Black Women Organized for Political Action. And, of course, there's the trailblazer Shirley Chisholm, who became the first African American woman in Congress in 1968 and the first woman and African American to seek the nomination for US president in 1972.[9]

And though I was introduced to feminist scholarship by white women, it was Joan Morgan's *When Chickenheads Come Home to Roost: A Hip-Hop Feminist Breaks It Down*, that made me feel that feminism was a movement I could call my own.

Once when I called myself a feminist in front of a woman that I deeply admired, she looked at me and said, "Feminist? What does that even mean?" And that's a fair question because even in the twenty-first century some people still believe being a feminist means you hate men. However, I'm pretty sure the man I've been married to for more than fifteen years would disagree. Some people think being a feminist means you're against motherhood, and while I am childfree by choice, and I do have a problem with people who believe a woman's worth should be tied to her uterus, I have the utmost respect for mothers, including stay-at-home moms. Others think being a feminist means hating makeup, dresses, or the color pink. But I am probably one of the girliest girls you will ever meet. Even my cell phone case is so girly it needs its own bra.

So, yes, I am a feminist, and that means I believe in the social, economic, and political equality of the sexes. But I am a modern feminist, I am a Black feminist, and that means my feminism is intersectional. My feminism recognizes that the women's movement cannot discuss issues of gender without also tackling issues of race, ethnicity, nationality, class, ability, sexual orientation, religion, age, and other elements of identity because they all intersect.

Some people think a label like "feminist" is unnecessary. After all, I can believe in equality and do work to bring about this equality without calling myself the f-word. But I am on a mission to destigmatize this word by wearing it proudly because when we stigmatize the title of the women's movement it is easier to ignore the issues this movement tries to bring to light. Silencing feminists makes it easier to silence any woman, whether she identifies as a feminist or not.

For me, feminism is not just political. It is personal. I am a feminist because I don't believe my worth is tied to the clothes in my closet or the number that looks back at me when I step on a scale. I am a feminist because even though I am happily married, I don't believe every woman's purpose in life is to be a wonderful wife and model mother. I am a feminist because one day my father told me I could be and do whatever I wanted, and I believed him.

And these things don't change simply because my skin is a darker shade of brown. In fact, there is a quote by the late African American poet June Jordan that reconciles being both feminist and a woman of color quite wonderfully:

> I am a feminist, and what that means to me is much the same as the meaning of the fact that I am Black: it means that I must undertake to love myself and to respect myself as though my very life depends upon self-love and self-respect.

Writing Prompts:
What does the word "feminist" mean to you?
Write about a woman from history you admire. How does she inspire you? What do you plan to do with this inspiration?

Why I Won't Shut Up about Being a Girl–or Being Black

Lady. Babe. Girl.

These are three of my favorite words, but some of my fellow feminists believe I should expunge them from my vocabulary. Yes, I am a feminist. Yes, I want equal pay, equal opportunities, and equal respect. This does not mean I want society to pretend I am not female.

In 2016, a widely read blog for female creatives wrote a eulogy for the popular hashtag "#girlboss." "Would a man ever call himself a boy boss?" the writer asked.

Probably not. But who said I was trying to do business like a man? A reader of my own blog, took offense when I called myself a lady writer and referred to my personal notebook as my lady journal.

Look. I get it. I understand that "girl," "lady," and "babe" are all words sometimes wielded against women as a verbal weapon to put us in "our place." But it was when I decided to reclaim and redefine these words for myself that I found the courage to take my place. I found the courage to take a seat at the table and, with all my girl power and lady might, flip the table over.

I don't call myself a girl boss so I will be less threatening to the male ego. I call myself a girl boss because I want you to know I can take your job while wearing pink and flipping my hair, if that's what I choose to do. This is why I won't shut up about being a girl. Furthermore, girl is the "root word in the unique love language between Black women, regardless of age," as Kenya Hunt states in her book *Girl Gurl Grrrl: On Womanhood and Belonging in the Age of Black Girl Magic.*[1]

I won't shut up about being a girl and I'm not going to shut up about being Black. My thoughts on gender are quite like my ideas on race. When someone tells me they don't see color, I simply do not believe them. If we are only friends because you don't see me as Black, we are not friends at all. Likewise, if you only respect me because I seem like "one of the boys," you don't respect me at all.

I am a woman, and I am Black. Those two aspects of my identity will always and forever intersect. My feminism is intersectional. And this also means I respect those who don't conform to society's idea that there are only two genders.

Another favorite phrase that came under fire back in 2016 was the ever-popular "Black girl magic." A writer for Elle magazine complained that "Black girl magic" perpetuates the "strong Black woman" archetype, which suggests that Black women can survive it all and withstand it all, a notion that causes many Black women to suffer in silence.[2] But many writers and cultural critics agree that Black girl magic is simply a celebration. "It's not about Black women being exclusive or being superhuman; it's about Black women recognizing the humanity in one another that so many others often fail to see," Demetria Lucas wrote for The Root in a response to the Elle essay.[3]

For me, Black girl magic isn't about unicorns, pixie dust, or even superhuman strength; it's about self-love.

I do not long for the day you no longer see me as a woman. I dream of the day when all expressions of gender—male, female, and beyond the binary—are honored.

I do not long for the day you no longer see me as Black. I dream of the day when all races and ethnicities are celebrated.

When I was diagnosed with cancer, I found myself facing a new set of rules attempting to regulate my words. "Release yourself from warrior language," I was told. "Don't say you're fighting cancer. You are healing from cancer."

I get it. I know that it's best to focus on loving your body instead of hating a disease. And each cancer patient has unique needs. But I knew to get through surgery, chemo, and radiation, I would need to picture myself at Madison Square Garden in the boxing ring squaring off with cancer like Muhammad Ali and Joe Frazier. Cancer may win the first fight, but I got best of three!

Fortunately, my friends and family know me well. My brother sent me memes labeling Mike Tyson as "Javacia" and Tyson's KO'd opponent "cancer." My friend Annemarie bought me miniature pink boxing gloves from the Muhammad Ali Center in Louisville.

My cousin Tasha, who's my best friend and more like a sister than a cousin, bought me a T-shirt and matching tote bag with the words "Fight Like a Girl." I wore that shirt and took my tote with me for my first day of chemo. I put on a brave face for my husband, but I was terrified. I had no idea how my body would react to the chemicals that were about to be pumped through my veins for the next five months.

But I know now that I don't have to be fearless to be fierce. I can feel the fear and do it anyway, as the saying goes. I can acknowledge that I'm afraid and not let fear keep me from living my best life. And that's what it means to fight like a girl.

My sister-in-law designed a personalized Funko POP! of me as Beyoncé armed with her Hot Sauce bat. The base of the doll's stand reads: "Cancer ... who the F**K do you think I is? You ain't messing with no AVERAGE chick, boy!!" Yes, that's the kind of energy, that's the kind of language I needed to bring to my breast cancer battle. And I will keep writing in my lady journal about my life as a girl boss to conjure my Black girl magic for the day.

Writing Prompts:

What does the word "girl" mean to you?
Write about a time you felt pressured to downplay a facet of your identity.

I'm Feeling Lucky–and Enraged

I called it my cancer journal. A pink notebook filled with empowering women's quotes and the words "The Future Is Female" on the cover. Yes, you still have a future, I'd whisper to myself whenever I saw the phrase. While undergoing treatments for breast cancer, I used this journal to count down how many doses of chemo and how many rounds of radiation I had left. I wrote down how I felt after each treatment and noted which foods made me feel sick and which didn't. I wrote down advice from the counselors and survivors I met in a virtual support group.

Most of all, I wrote down questions. So. Many. Questions. Questions for my nurses. Questions for my oncologists. Questions for my surgeon.

When it comes to health care, I've always been lucky. My lupus diagnosis in 2008 didn't come after spending years visiting doctor after doctor, searching for answers to questions of chronic pain. I mentioned my fatigue, achy joints, vitiligo spots, and bouts of Raynaud's disease to my primary care physician at the time as casually as someone rattling off a grocery list. She looked at me and said, "We need to test you for lupus."

Years later, in a new state with a new doctor, I once again had a proactive primary care doc who urged me to get a mammogram, even though I was in my thirties. It's true that women in their twenties and thirties account for only about five percent of breast cancer cases. But it's the most common cancer for women in this age group. Breast cancer is often diagnosed in its later stages for women under forty, which means the survival rate is lower and the recurrence rate is higher.[1] And while Black women and white women get breast cancer at about the same rate, Black women are more likely to be diagnosed before age 45 and, regardless of age, Black women die from breast cancer at a higher rate than white women.[2]

Even when I was diagnosed with breast cancer at age thirty-eight, and even after I learned I'd need chemo, I still felt lucky. I felt lucky that I had insurance that covered my treatment. I felt lucky that whenever I said I was in pain, my doctors and nurses believed me and scrambled to do something about it. And I felt lucky that they would answer every question in my little pink book.

I felt lucky because in 2020, thirty million people were uninsured, and about half of those were people of color, according to The Brookings Institution, a research and public policy organization in Washington, DC.[3] I felt lucky because both anecdotal evidence and published studies reveal that many medical professionals don't take Black people's pain seriously. According to a 2016 study published in the Proceedings of the National Academy of Science, half the medical students surveyed had false beliefs such as "black people's skin is thicker than white people's." And trainees who believed that Black people are not as sensitive to pain as white people were less likely to treat Black people's pain appropriately.[4]

The staggering Black maternal mortality rates show that this type of implicit bias can be deadly. According to the CDC, each year about seven hundred people in the United States die during pregnancy or the year after. Black women are three times more likely to die from a pregnancy-related cause than white women.[5] I feel lucky, and I feel angry because I shouldn't feel lucky! Affordable health care and being listened to and taken seriously by your doctors should be the norm for everyone.

I will use my privilege and my platform to try to do something about this. I've written stories about the Black Maternal Health Momnibus Act, which seeks to use legislation to address every aspect of the maternal health crisis in America.[6] And I've written about the CDC's Hear Her campaign, which seeks to improve communication between patients and their doctors and help to make healthcare providers, patients, and their families more aware of the warning signs of potentially life-threatening complications.[7] I've had the chance to be a voice for other breast cancer patients of color in sessions with healthcare providers thanks to the work of organizations like the Tigerlily Foundation, which provides breast cancer education, awareness, advocacy and support for women ages 15 to 45, with a focus on women of color.[8]

Even though I'm a writer, sometimes words aren't enough. The Black women who are suffering and not getting the care that they deserve need more than the empowering quotes in my pink cancer journal. So, I will keep writing, but I also will keep fighting.

Writing Prompts:

What are the causes that keep you up at night? How can you use your writing to raise awareness? What else can you do to help bring about change?

This Is What a Feminist Writer Looks Like

I started my professional writing career at an alternative weekly in Louisville, where I worked as a features reporter and wrote a biweekly column. In my column, I often examined women's issues and quickly earned the reputation as the paper's go-to girl for all things feminism.

One day, a young woman from another department came to our office to discuss an idea she had for a women's empowerment project, and she walked directly to the female reporter who sat in the cubicle next to mine. "I've heard you write a lot about feminism, and that it's really important to you," she said to my colleague. Everyone in the office stared at the young woman in confusion. Then my colleague pointed to me and said, "Javacia writes about women's issues. Not me."

The look of shock on the young woman's face indirectly told me what I had been told explicitly many times before: "You don't look like a feminist!" I've been told I don't look like a feminist because I'm Black. "A Black woman can't be a feminist," I was told via email after I wrote a piece on feminism and natural hair for a popular beauty blog for women of color. "A Black woman shouldn't be a feminist," I was told by a Louisville resident who couldn't believe I would associate myself with a movement started by "wealthy, racist white women."

But I suspect that the woman from my old job wasn't confused by the color of my skin. She was most likely perplexed by the color of my outfit. When this woman came to our office in search of the resident feminist, she didn't bother asking anyone to point her in the right direction. She went straight to my coworker, who only dressed in neutral colors, never wore makeup or heels, and chose not to shave her underarms or legs. Meanwhile, I was probably wearing pastel and pumps. I'm sure my eyeshadow was perfectly color-coordinated with my outfit, and my cubicle looked like the color pink had thrown up all over it.

Though I think today's young feminists are dismantling this notion, in the past there has been an assumption that a woman can't be both feminist and feminine. And all women—even those who don't identify as feminist—should want to do away with this idea. (I realize that how we define "feminine" is a social construct that needs to be examined, but that's another topic for another book.)

In her 2013 HelloGiggles.com article "Feminist or Feminine? Oh Wait, They Aren't Mutually Exclusive," Julia Gazdag wrote, "The idea that women cannot express their femininity and be autonomous is really saying that women must emulate men to have a voice."[1] Women are often made to feel that to be taken seriously in the workplace, and even within the feminist community, we must de-emphasize our femaleness.

Nigerian writer Chimamanda Ngozi Adichie addressed this in her 2012 TED Talk, "We Should All Be Feminists," that later permeated pop culture after being featured in Beyoncé's hit song "***Flawless." Adichie shared that the first time she taught a college-level writing class she wore a "very manly and very ugly suit" instead of the "girly skirt" and "shiny lip gloss" she wanted to wear. She made this choice, she says, because she thought her students wouldn't respect her if she looked too feminine. Adichie wishes she hadn't worn that ugly suit. She says, "Had I then had the confidence I have now to be myself, my students would have benefited even more from my teaching because I would have been more comfortable and more fully and truly myself."[2]

Allow me to pause and acknowledge that women who, like my former colleague, shirk conventional beauty standards face much criticism and judgment and absolutely need support from people who believe women should have a right to dress their bodies however they choose. But just as my fellow feminists would (and should) defend my former colleague's choice to not shave or sport girly getup, they should also support my choice to paint my nails. In the women's movement of the 1970s, some feminists embraced a so-called masculine aesthetic to challenge conventional notions of beauty and femininity. Today, plenty of women continue to follow their example, not necessarily to make a political statement, but simply because these are the clothes in which they are most comfortable.

These are very valid choices but so is my decision to wear polka dots or pink. I wear sundresses and pencil skirts in the summer for the same reason I wear jeans and blazers when the weather turns cold—because I want to, not because I feel as if I have to in order to be attractive or a real woman. My fashion choices are just that: my choices.

Telling a woman she does or does not look like a feminist is problematic because it implies there is a feminist aesthetic. The purpose of feminism is to strive for the social, political, and economic equality of the sexes, not to construct an image of the ideal woman. If someone tells me one day that I do look like a feminist, I hope the comment has nothing to do with my couture and everything to do with my confidence.

The Story of an Outfit

In my next writing life, I want to be a fashion blogger. I want a website that boasts bold and beautiful photos of me sporting chic and trendy outfits paired with poems about my life or essays on the importance of women having a strong sense of their personal style. But there's one huge obstacle preventing me from realizing this dream: I hate shopping. I know there's a stereotype that shopping is the favorite hobby of all double X chromosome carriers, but I'm here to tell you that stereotype is a lie. So, whenever I realize I need a new outfit for some special occasion, my heart sinks.

For example, in late 2014 I found out I had been selected as one of my city's Top Forty under Forty by the *Birmingham Business Journal.* When I found out I had been picked the first thought that came to mind was, "Crap! I have nothing to wear for the photo shoot!" Don't judge me. Yes, I also thought about what an amazing honor this was.

I felt grateful that someone cared enough about the work I do through See Jane Write to nominate me for this recognition. To have my peers and a publication like the *Birmingham Business Journal* recognize See Jane Write as a real business meant the world to me. Everything about this had to be perfect—especially the outfit I wore in the photo to accompany my article. This meant I'd have to have a run-in with retail. Surprisingly, the outfit I'd buy for this photo shoot would teach me some of the most important business lessons I've ever learned.

This outfit taught me the importance of asking for help. One of my friends—we'll call her Dee—loves shopping just about as much as I hate it. She hits the mall nearly every weekend. We once took a girls' trip to Atlanta and when we walked into Lenox Square, she told me she got goosebumps. I got a stomachache. After browsing one store, I was ready to go. She could have perused the shops from open to close.

So I knew exactly who to call for help with this outfit. She took me to Banana Republic, Ann Taylor Loft, and White House Black Market before we finally settled on my look: a winter white Olivia Pope–inspired blazer atop an embellished cream-colored bustier with black ankle pants and black stilettos. Dee added a statement necklace, which took me out of my comfort zone

(I hardly ever wear necklaces) but was just what the outfit needed to take it to the next level.

Likewise, in business, I've had to learn to ask for help. I had to let go of the notion that I have to (or that I'm able to) do everything myself. I started working with business coaches and marketing strategists to take See Jane Write to the next level and make it an even better resource for women writers, bloggers, and entrepreneurs.

When the "Top Forty under Forty" article appeared in print and online, friends, family members, and even complete strangers were raving about my picture. One friend said, "You look fabulous, professional, creative, interesting, fierce, adorable, and approachable! How did you do that?" And with that, she summed up exactly what I'd hoped the outfit would convey. But I almost didn't wear it.

Near the end of my shopping trip with Dee, I started to second-guess myself and started thinking that I should just wear a traditional black business suit so that my fellow honorees and others would take me seriously. But then I realized how I was failing to practice what I preach about the importance of embracing femininity and not treating it like a liability. This outfit reminded me of the importance of being myself.

Since I started See Jane Write, several other writing and blogging networks have been developed in Birmingham and surrounding areas, and they're all fantastic. At first, I was tempted to closely watch and attempt to mimic what they were doing and how. Then I realized that tactic was just silly. See Jane Write has been successful because I respond to the questions and concerns of my members, and I will continue to do just that. I will stay true to my mission. I will stay true to myself—and try to look fabulous while doing so.

But I probably will never be a fashion blogger.

Writing Prompts:

What is the story behind your favorite outfit?
Write your style statement. What do you want your wardrobe to convey about who you are?

Hair Story

Every Black woman has a hair story. Mine is one with many different acts. When I was younger, I hated my hair even though everyone around me seemed obsessed with it. They all said that I had "good hair," though I didn't see what was so great about it. They declared it would be a sin to ever cut it.

"Your hair is your glory," the old church ladies would tell me.

To me, my hair was just dumb. It was ridiculously long, impossibly thick, and perpetually frizzy. My mom wouldn't let me get a relaxer like all the other Black girls at school, but I was determined to have straight hair come hell or high water. And hell did come in the form of the hours I spent trying to wrestle my unruly curls into submission with the strongest, hottest hair appliances I could afford.

Growing up, my hair brought me a lot of unwanted attention like the lingering eyes of men old enough to be my father or girls refusing to be my friend and whispering, "She think she all that cuz she got long hair." But nothing was as embarrassing as the day in middle school when a guest speaker in my social studies class pointed to me and announced to everyone in the room that had I been a slave, "Massa" would've taken one look at my hair and decided to have his way with me—repeatedly. After that day, I started wearing my hair in a bun and wrapping it in a wide headband to make sure my locks didn't break loose.

I didn't start wearing my hair down again regularly until college and only after I cut off several inches. I was still struggling to keep my mane bone straight. Then one summer day when I was twenty-one, while on my third hour of doing my hair, my roommate turned to me and said, "Maybe your hair doesn't want to be straight. Why don't you just wear it curly?"

Never before had anyone suggested that letting my hair exist in its naturally curly state was an option. But in that moment, something clicked and just like that, I started rocking my curls. Keep in mind that this was years before natural hair was cool. So most people–especially my family members–wanted to tie me down and run a hot comb through my hair. But I was unbothered and wrote love poems to my hair, which turned into love poems to myself. The more I accepted my hair as is, the more I learned to accept myself.

Eventually, natural hair would become all the rage. The same people who used to ask, "Don't you want a perm?" were now asking me for curly hair care product suggestions. As a journalist, I started writing about the natural hair movement and how Black women were redefining beauty standards.

Going natural made me a better feminist, too, because it pushed me to think about all of my beauty and fashion choices. When I did decide, years later, to get my hair professionally and temporarily straightened, I was sure to check myself. Why am I doing this? Is it because I think hair must be straight to be pretty as I did when I was younger? After some soul searching, I was sure that wasn't my motivation. When I would straighten my hair, it was usually because I was bored and wanted a different look for a couple of weeks or because I wanted to wear a cute hat that wouldn't fit over my curly coif.

I started asking myself other questions. Why am I wearing these clothes? Why am I putting on this makeup? Am I doing this because I truly want to or because I feel like I have to in order to be accepted or loved? Those are the kinds of questions I ask myself to keep my motives in check, but those are questions I didn't start asking until I went natural.

But the saga continues. Eventually, my hair became my feminist fashion statement not because of its curliness but because of its color. I started graying when I was still in my twenties. While I didn't yet boast a full head of gray hair like beauties Ty Alexander or Tennille Murphy, my silver streak got plenty of attention.

At first, I made jokes about the irony of having gray hair and a baby face. "Who am I? Benjamin Button!" I'd say to friends. But I never once thought of dyeing my hair. Silver hair meant I could be Storm for Halloween without buying a wig. I was one step closer to being one of the X-Men!

Then the comments started. "Girl, why you got all that gray hair in your head? Ain't you young?" asked the rude cashier at Walgreens. "You need to stop letting life stress you out. That's why you have all that gray hair," said a "concerned" family member. And the most annoying comment of all: "You're so brave!" Apparently sporting gray hair was enough to be the Angela Davis of my generation.

At first, I was confused. I wondered: if my gray hair wasn't bothering me, why was it bothering everybody else? Then I got angry. Why won't they all just shut up?! But, to borrow a phrase from Tamara Winfrey-Harris, I realized I was hating the player and ignoring the game.

Society teaches us that signs of aging should be avoided at all costs because each wrinkle, each silver strand of hair, suggests you are one day closer to becoming obsolete. We women especially are taught that once we're a certain age we are too old to wear stylish clothes, have great sex, or go after our dreams. So, of course, my friends would expect me to dye my hair!

But I am determined to be fierce and fabulous in my forties, fifties, and beyond. I'm going to write about every adventure to encourage other women with ageless ambition to do what they want, when they want, while wearing what they want. Just as embracing my curly hair helped me love the woman I am, embracing my gray hair has helped me be excited about the woman I am to become.

Writing Prompts:

What's your hair story?
Write a story about getting unwanted attention.

I Am Not My Hair

"Javacia—the girl with the long, pretty hair."

That's how people have described me for most of my life. As I got older and started making a name for myself as a writer, blogger, business owner, and teacher, I thought this would change. And in some ways, it did. In some circles, I'm "the blogger girl." Some people actually call me "See Jane Write." And because I taught English for ten years, to my former students I will always be "Mrs. Bowser."

But for most people, I just went from being "the *girl* with the long, pretty hair" to "the *lady* with the long, pretty hair." I know I should have been flattered. Someone saying my hair is pretty is a compliment. But I was tired of people paying more attention to my hair than to me.

On May 7, 2020, I started chemotherapy for breast cancer, and by the end of the month I'd lost my "long, pretty hair." But even in its absence, my hair continued to steal the show. I'll be honest, before starting chemo I worried about how it would feel to lose my hair. I wondered if I'd cry or feel ugly or feel like less of a woman. I wondered if I'd hate looking in the mirror. But none of that happened.

On the evening of May 24–after realizing my hair had shed so much it was too tangled to comb–I cut my hair down to just an inch or two. I wasn't sad at all. My attitude was this: let me cut this mess off and get on with my day. This happened less than an hour before I had to do a Facebook Live broadcast. I just threw on a headwrap and went on with the show.

When the rest of my hair started to fall out, I still wasn't sad. I thought I'd look at myself in the mirror, see the last stubborn strands clinging to my scalp and feel ashamed. But I didn't. Instead, I felt fascinated. I felt like I was seeing myself for the first time—like the real me had been hiding beneath my mane for all those years. I looked in the mirror and whispered, "There you are."

However, many of my friends and family were devastated that my signature curls were gone. They assumed I was just as heartbroken as they were. But here's the thing—while hair loss is the most visible side effect of chemotherapy, for many cancer patients, it is the least of our concerns.

Early in my treatment, my red blood cell count dropped so dramatically my doctor thought I might need a blood transfusion. My heart rate was often so high I could see my heart beating through my chest. I was still able to walk for exercise every day, but sometimes walking for thirty minutes felt like walking for thirty miles.

Fortunately, I didn't vomit at all, but I felt queasy pretty much every minute of every day. I lost fifteen pounds in one month because some days rice and applesauce were the only things I could stand to eat. Some days everything tasted like sand.

Neuropathy and hand-foot syndrome are other common side effects of chemotherapy. Some mornings, I would wake up and could barely use my hands. Nonetheless, my oncologist and nurses all said that I tolerated chemotherapy very well. And I must say that my good days did outweigh my bad days. I was able to write, work, and walk in spite of everything. I can honestly say I wasn't just surviving chemo; I was thriving.

I used my blog to share the other side of the chemo side effects. And I didn't share these details because I wanted pity. The idea of people feeling sorry for me bothered me more than the fact that my stomach couldn't handle queso during treatment. I shared my story to urge people to stop being so concerned with how a person looks that they ignore how that person feels. Likewise, let's not be so concerned with a woman's appearance that we overlook the work she does or the kind of person she strives to be.

How I Lost and Found Confidence After Cancer

Originally Published October 2020 on ReckonSouth.com. Reprinted with permission.

I miss my eyebrows.

When I started chemotherapy in early May of 2020 to treat stage two breast cancer, I knew that by the end of the month I would start to lose my hair. I worried about how this would affect my self-esteem and even my identity. All my life I've been "the girl with the long, pretty hair." I thought that after losing my hair, I'd lose my sense of self. But when I lost my hair, I didn't cry or even feel sad. I was just annoyed because I was cleaning up hair all the time. In fact, thanks to my extensive collection of head wraps and scarves (cancer, but make it fashion!) I still felt cute!

But here's the thing–eventually chemo takes *all* of your hair. Eventually, you lose hair everywhere. Yes, even there. #freebrazilian. And when I lost my eyebrows, everything changed. When I lost my eyebrows, I no longer felt cute. I already didn't feel sexy. When actual poison is being pumped into your body, it's hard to see yourself as a sexual being. Instead, you see yourself as a toxic landfill. And once I lost my eyebrows, I didn't want to see myself at all. In the process of killing cancer, chemotherapy killed my confidence too—at first.

But then something unexpected happened.

One day I was scrolling through pictures in my phone and as I saw the old me, I realized I had no desire to be her again. Yes, pre-cancer Javacia (or Javacia B.C. as I call her) had full eyebrows. Yes, she had long, thick, curly hair. But present-day Javacia has an outlook on life that the old me didn't.

Pre-cancer Javacia constantly worried about how she looked. She worried about her muffin top and her double chin. She worried about cellulite and wobbly arms. She worried about reaching her goal weight before her fortieth birthday. But present-day Javacia finds such concerns laughable.

I know that after surgery, chemo, and radiation, my body will never be the same again. I know I will never have what society and media consider a perfect body. But that frees me to love the body I have just as it is.

Some cancer patients long for the days when they will have the capacity to sweat the small stuff again. And I get that. But I hope my IDGAF attitude lasts long after my active cancer treatment has ended.

Am I saying I'm glad I got cancer? Hell no! If given a choice I would most definitely opt out. But cancer has changed me in a way that I don't think anything else could have.

One day I was chatting with a breast cancer survivor, and she told me that when she looks back on the year she went through chemotherapy and radiation she can't help but think, "I'm a G! I did that!"

That's when I realized that pre-cancer Javacia was strong, but present-day Javacia is a total badass. While dealing with surgeries and chemo side effects I've landed several new freelance gigs, had several virtual speaking engagements, and grown the See Jane Write community. And I've walked for exercise for at least thirty minutes every single day–including the day of my lumpectomy.

Cancer has also taught me to stop tethering my worth to my productivity. Overall, my body tolerated chemo very well, according to my oncologist and nurses. But losing my hair and my eyebrows just scratched the surface of side effects. I've had to deal with nausea, loss of appetite, neuropathy, hand-foot syndrome, and much more.

Some days I couldn't write because I couldn't even use my hands. Some days I couldn't brainstorm business ideas because I was so tired. Some days I had to sleep for more than twelve hours. But those moments taught me to stop behaving as if I have to earn love. Those moments taught me that I am worthy of love and joy and all good things simply because I am. I've learned that I can take a break, and my world won't break into pieces.

Armed with all of these lessons, I am more confident today than I've ever been in my life–even though I don't have eyebrows. I'm not saying I look in the mirror and think to myself, "You are beautiful because you are strong." I look in the mirror and think, "You look like a Teenage Mutant Ninja Turtle."

The makeup tutorial I had at Sephora last year has come in handy and I do a great job drawing on my eyebrows every day. Thanks to my makeup bag and headscarf collection, people are always raving about how great I look when I go live on Facebook or post current photos to Instagram. And I appreciate each compliment, but I want to tell them, I did not wake up like this. I woke up looking like Donatello. No, I still don't feel pretty. But cancer has taught me that pretty is overrated.

On Walking and Writing

In 2014, I started a tradition of challenging myself each summer to walk/run one hundred miles in thirty days. This was a terrible idea. I live in Alabama, which means that in the summer it's ninety degrees, in the shade, before breakfast. Until 2019, I was a teacher, so summer should've meant an opportunity to sleep in and not set the dreaded morning alarm. But because of this silly goal of mine, I had to rise at dawn to get in my daily miles without risking having a heat stroke.

On top of that, I have lupus, which makes my joints hurt and my skin sensitive to the sun. My previous rheumatologist told me I should not run at all. But I got a second opinion and soon began this tradition that each summer leaves me with sore muscles, blisters on my toes, and the worst racer-back tan lines you have ever seen. Check my Google history in the summer, and you'll see I search for "how to get rid of tan lines" more than anything else.

You may be wondering why I keep setting this goal for myself each year when it seems that the only gold medals waiting for me at the finish line are the aforementioned ailments. Do I lose weight when I go after this goal? Sometimes, but that's not my motivation at all. Believe it or not, achieving my goal to walk/run one hundred miles in thirty days boosts my confidence as a writer.

If you're a writer, I believe you will gain the confidence you need to go after your goals if you stop dwelling on the things you haven't done and start celebrating the things that you have—even if those things aren't writing-related. It's OK if you didn't get a book deal by thirty or make the *New York Times* bestseller list by forty. It doesn't matter if your blog has yet to land you a commercial or a five-figure campaign with your favorite brand. If you're a single mom who's raised an amazing kid all by yourself then, of course, you can successfully self-publish a book. If you've trained for and completed a marathon, of course, you have the discipline to blog.

You may be wondering why I chose to run these one hundred miles in the summer. Why not opt for milder months? As I mentioned, I used to be a teacher, so it was during the summer that I had the most free time. So that's when I decided to run, even if running conditions were less than ideal. There's a lesson here too.

If you're serious about making your dream a reality, regardless of what that dream may be, you must be willing to do the work even in the midst of crappy conditions. Writers, for example, need to be willing to write whenever, wherever. One friend of mine wrote her latest book while waiting in her kid's carpool line. Another worked on her blog while pumping breast milk. If they can do that, I can get up early to run on the hotel gym treadmill while I'm on vacation. And if I can walk/run one hundred miles every summer in spite of a medical condition that tells me I shouldn't be able to, then I can do anything else I want to do too.

Eventually, I decided to give my joints a bit of break and started doing more walking than running. But I still wanted a challenge. So on January 1, 2020, I resolved to walk for exercise for at least thirty minutes every day for 366 days. Then on January 24, I was diagnosed with breast cancer. The goal digger in me must confess that when I got the news, one of my first thoughts was, "Crap! Is this going to mess up my plans to walk every day?"

Spoiler alert–it didn't.

I walked after my lumpectomy, taking slow and tiny steps in front of my house with my husband by my side. I walked after surgery for my chemotherapy port placement. I walked after my first dose of chemotherapy.

As my chemo treatments progressed, walking got harder and harder. Walking for thirty minutes felt like walking for thirty miles. My heart was always racing like I was doing a CrossFit cardio workout of the day. The soles of my feet ached from hand-foot syndrome, a side effect of the chemo drug Taxol. But I kept walking.

Some of the people who followed my #seejavaciawalk Instagram stories called me a warrior. Some called me crazy. My oncologist actually recommended that I exercise every day for at least twenty minutes while going through chemo to help fight fatigue. But to be honest, I didn't keep walking through cancer for any of the physical health benefits. I didn't walk to fight fatigue or to lose weight or even for cardiovascular health. I walked for my mental health. I walked to stay sane. And I still do.

Cancer, chemo, and all of the side effects of both can make me feel as if I have no control over my own body. Lupus (and the joint pain that comes with it) can make me feel that way too. But when I walk, I take back my power. When I walk, I take back my agency over my own body. When I walk, I feel free. In October of 2020, I was quoted in an article in *O magazine* about how cancer patients were coping with treatment during the pandemic. As I explained in the interview, when I walk, I feel like myself–even if just for a little while.

And yes, I still believe walking helps my writing. In fact, I'm so obsessed with the topic of walking and writing I should write a book on it. Duncan Minshull did.[1] In his book *Beneath My Feet: Writers on Walking,* Minshull includes a letter that Danish philosopher *Søren* Kierkegaard wrote to his niece in 1847. In it he declares:

> Above all, do not lose your desire to walk: every day I walk myself into a state of well-being and walk away from every illness; I have walked myself into my best thoughts, and I know of no thought so burdensome that one cannot walk away from it.

Those words could have been my mantra in 2020. In addition to faith, family, and friends, the things that got me through cancer were walking and writing. And therefore, I believe I can walk and write my way through anything. I am convinced that walking and writing go hand in hand.

Lots of famous writers like Charles Dickens and Ernest Hemingway loved taking daily walks. In 1851, Henry David Thoreau delivered an entire lecture on walking at the Concord Lyceum.[2] And in *The Awakening*, one of my favorite novels of all time, Kate Chopin writes "I always feel so sorry for women who don't like to walk; they miss so much—so many rare little glimpses of life…"

Both walking and writing can boost your health. That's why many health care professionals, from medical doctors to psychotherapists, recommend writing as a way for patients to heal ailments of both mind and body. Journaling every day can help you manage anxiety, reduce stress, and cope with depression.[3]

Meanwhile, walking is the most underrated form of exercise[4] and deserves so much more praise than it gets. According to Healthline.com, walking just thirty minutes a day can help do the following:

- strengthen your heart
- lower your blood sugar
- ease joint pain
- boost immune function
- boost energy
- improve your mood[5]

And the toned legs you can get from walking daily are nice incentives too! Of course, you should talk to your doctor before starting any new exercise regimen if you're not sure you're healthy enough to walk.

Another reason I'm convinced that walking can make you a better writer—science says so. A study from Stanford University found that creative thinking improves while walking and shortly thereafter.[6] This works whether you're walking inside or outdoors. Apparently, it's the act of walking itself, not the environment, that can get your muse moving.[7] Perhaps that's why I always get inspired to write while I'm walking. You'll often see me take my phone from my pocket mid-walk to thumb out ideas in my Notes app.

If you're struggling to find time to write every day, the idea of trying to walk every day, too, might seem impossible. But I believe that taking time to walk can actually help you find time to write. Let me explain.

When I set out to walk every day for 366 days, I prioritized this goal. This meant that each night as I sat down with my Day Designer to plan the next day, I would schedule when I was going to go for my walk. And I would treat this time like an appointment that I couldn't miss. We must do the same thing with writing. Prioritize your writing goals. Be intentional and schedule time to work on your writing goals every day or at least five hours a week.

Remember that with both walking and writing, you don't have to set out for a marathon. Just as walking only thirty minutes a day can improve your health, writing just five hundred words a day can help you finish that book you want to publish. Writing in your journal a little bit every night can help build enough material for that blog you want to launch.

During my cancer treatments, during my quest to walk every day for 366 days, I had the privilege of watching a Facebook Live discussion between GirlTrek, Nikki Giovanni, and Angela Davis. In the talk, Davis shared that she walks for exercise every day too. I was so excited to learn this. It felt like confirmation that my goal was a good idea. During the talk, Davis left us with a charge: "Walk in the direction of freedom." I believe that when you walk for the sake of both your wellness and your writing, you're doing exactly that.

Writing Prompts:

Write about your favorite way to move your body.

The next time you're facing writer's block, move your body. Go for a walk if you're physically able to do so. Afterward, write a journal entry about how the movement made you feel.

Body Paragraphs

When I was a size four, I chastised my body for not being a size two. And despite wanting to be a size two, I also wanted curves. For years I stood in the mirror cursing a waistline that wouldn't shrink, and breasts that wouldn't grow.

Then in 2000, I became a group fitness instructor at my university's recreation center. I'd lace up my sneakers and put on my microphone and I'd feel like a superhero thwarting the evil villain called low self-esteem. I loved my legs each time they helped me lead a step aerobics class. I loved my arms each time I did push-ups—fifty of them, with no breaks. The size of my clothes didn't matter nearly as much as how long I could hold my planks. It didn't matter if I only wore a B-cup-sized bra. When I was teaching dance aerobics classes, I felt '90s era Janet Jackson sexy.

Because of these group fitness classes, I stopped obsessing over what my body looked like and started focusing on what it could do. I was convinced I'd found the answer to loving oneself. Then, in 2008, I was diagnosed with lupus.

When my doctor first said, "I think we should test you for lupus," the words seemed to flop through the air like a bird with a broken wing before landing in my lap. Then I shook off the shock and simply laughed. I couldn't have lupus. I was fine. Sure, I had mysterious rashes on my face and my arms, but I figured they were from some unknown allergy. And yes, my knees, shoulders, wrists, ankles, and elbows ached like those of an eighty-year-old woman despite the fact I was only twenty-six at the time, but I figured it was from all those years of teaching fitness classes.

I knew I was tired all the time, but that was simply because I needed more sleep, I thought. These things were not happening to me because of lupus. I didn't know much about lupus, but I knew I didn't have it.

I was wrong.

Lupus, a chronic autoimmune disease that can damage any part of the body, including the skin, joints, and major organs such as the heart, lungs, kidneys, and brain, is a confusing disease because it has so many symptoms and affects each person differently.[1] Some common symptoms include joint and muscle pain, skin rashes, extreme fatigue, and anemia. Lupus can be mild to life-threatening. According to the Lupus Foundation of America (LFA), one in four people with lupus receives disability benefits.[2] For some, lupus manifests itself in joint and muscle pain, fatigue, and occasional skin rashes. For many others, it can mean kidney failure.[1]

So far, my lupus has been mild to moderate. My doctors can't say with certainty whether or not my lupus will get worse. In the meantime, I am thankful for each day that it hasn't.

On good days, I write, run, and spend time with my husband and friends with no trouble at all. On bad days, my joint and muscle pain can be so severe I can't lift a plate of food or a full glass. I can't lift my arms above my head, and I have trouble pushing myself off the side of the bed. And on my bad days, I forget to be grateful and instead I am cruel. I'm cruel to my body, scolding it for not being able to do all the things I want it to do.

After delivering the diagnosis, my doctor said to me: "You don't have to be afraid of this. You don't have to go around declaring the wolf is at your door."

But with those words, a war was waged. No, I would not fear this disease. But lupus, from the Latin word for wolf, had to become the big bad wolf because I needed something to fight. I had to turn lupus into the big bad wolf because the writer in me needed this metaphor. But in this story, I'm not a piglet. I am a house. The wolf can huff and puff and try to blow me down, but I am brick and mortar.

Lupus is a punk of a disease that loves to pick on Black and Brown women. Women of color—African Americans, Hispanics/Latinos, Asians, Native Americans, Alaska Natives, Native Hawaiians, and other Pacific Islanders— are two to three times more likely to be diagnosed with the disease than white women.[2] And research from The Michigan Lupus Epidemiology and Surveillance Program found that lupus affects one in 537 young African American women.[3]

Sometimes lupus was a redneck racist; sometimes a mouth-breathing misogynist. Every ache and every rash became a reminder of every time I've been told I couldn't or shouldn't do something because I am Black or because I am female. Eventually, all my metaphors would fail me. Eventually, I would realize that the only way to deal with the pain of lupus would be not to hate the disease but to love my body–even when it hurts, even when it's covered in rashes, even when it can't move the way I want it to move.

On September 17, 2017, I attended a two-hour body positivity workshop that was part group discussion, part yoga class. The instructor was Melissa Scott, a member of the See Jane Write community and the author of the book *White Girl in Yoga Pants: Stories of Yoga, Feminism and Inner Strength.*

"What does it mean to love your body?" Melissa asked us. We gave cliché answers about exercising and eating right, but Melissa challenged us to go deeper. She told us that to truly love our bodies we need to have a relationship with our bodies, a relationship much like the one we would have with a spouse or romantic partner.

Because I love my husband, I listen to him. I know what he likes and what he doesn't like because I pay attention. Because I love my husband, I support him, encouraging him to keep going when he faces challenges but never pushing him too far, ever ready to be his rest and reprieve when he needs it. Because I love my husband, I celebrate him for who he is as he is. How awful it would be to miss this chance to honor him as he is while longing for him to be something else, someone else.

If I love my body, I will listen to her. I will figure out what foods she likes and doesn't like. I will pay attention to the types of exercise that challenge my body the way she needs to be challenged without pushing her too far. If I love my body, I will give her rest. If I love my body, I will celebrate her as she is. My love won't be contingent on her size or even her strength. I will love her because she is mine, and I am hers.

Melissa then gave each of us paper and a pen for us to write our thoughts.

Sitting on the floor of the yoga studio, I wrote a love letter to my body. Perhaps it's more accurate to say I wrote vows, a promise to have and to hold her, for better, for worse, in sickness and in health, to love and to cherish her, till death do us part.

***

To My Beloved Body,

You are the love of my life. I am so thankful for every move you make to aid me in the pursuit of my dreams. I will spend the rest of my life showing you my gratitude.

I promise to celebrate you. I promise to praise you. I promise to accept you for who you are.

I promise to challenge you to make you stronger. I promise to hold you when you are weak.

I promise you cake and ice cream, but not too much.

I will clothe you in fine linen and purple yet acknowledge your nakedness as sacred beauty.

Together we will work hard but play harder.

Together we will dance, we will run, we will rest.

Together we will have the time of our lives.

Love,

J.

My Body, My Home

Poets who are more talented than I have written riveting works declaring that your body is your home. But after cancer, I feel evicted.

After cancer, my body doesn't feel like my home anymore. With every surgery and every treatment and even simple checkups, I feel as if my spirit floats up into the corner of the room's ceiling to watch–from afar—as this brown body is poked and prodded and poisoned. One day while in the shower I look down and whisper, "How can I ever trust you again?"

I turn to words for help. I read some rupi kaur and this inspires me to try to write my body a love poem. But it's just a litany of questions:

Why didn't you at least give me a warning? You gave me no sign that something was wrong!

Is this how my husband feels when I'm angry with him and he has no idea why?

Was this payback for that summer I drank too much?

Were you mad about all those late nights and early mornings? I only worked so hard so that we could have a better life!

I stop writing because now I sound like a guilty parent. I go for a walk because this is the one time during the day when my body and I are at peace. For me walking is moving meditation. As my feet pound the pavement, my wandering spirit starts to settle down.

Later, I try writing the poem again but find myself staring at a blinking cursor. Maybe I need to write this in longhand, I think. But then my journal taunts me with an empty page.

Good writers read good writing. I say this a lot to the women writers that I coach. So I decide I need to read more of another writer's words before I can write my own. I read Erin Hanson's poem "Your Home/You're Home," and I start weeping. As she writes of the body's broken windows and tear-stained floors, I remember the nights during treatment, when I would fall apart in my own arms. But I also find hope between the lines as Hanson's words remind me of the love and laughter in my life and of the dreams that even chemo couldn't kill.

I still haven't been able to write a love poem for my body, but I felt my body tell me that's okay. She wants me back anyway. So I stand in the shower, look down and say, "I'm home."

Writing Prompts:

Write a love letter to your body.
Write a love letter from your body.

Where I'm From

I am from laundromats with pinball, Pac-Man,
and Donkey Kong arcade games
I am from alleys littered with dirty needles and broken glass
I am from the trees too tall for the other girls in the neighborhood to climb
I am from fish sticks and potted meat
I am from honeysuckle and fireflies

I am from Easter dresses and knee-high socks
I am from my cousin's hand-me-downs
I am from the card table flipped over after you reneged in a game of Spades
I am from the bottom of Daddy's bottle of whiskey
From his aching back after another sixteen-hour workday

I am from playtime with Mama
From paper dolls and Easy-Bake ovens

I am from Granny's rice pudding and Sunday paper
From her cup of coffee, sugar, and cream
I am from Tang, lemonade, and sweet tea

I am from the Lord, who is my Shepherd,

Who tells me not to want, who tries to restore my soul.

Proud to Be a Southern-Fried Feminist

I often refer to myself as a Southern-fried feminist. It's a cute catchphrase I coined to describe my attempt to reconcile my Southern values with my feminist ideals. For years I've viewed my feminism and my Southern pride as two opposing forces struggling to peacefully coexist.

But I had it all wrong. "Southern feminist" is not an oxymoron or a contradiction. In fact, I have realized that my Southern roots don't make me a bad feminist. They make me a better one.

Southern feminists were embracing intersectionality long before it became a buzzword. Professor Kimberle Crenshaw, who coined the term, defined it as "the view that women experience oppression in varying configurations and in varying degrees of intensity. Cultural patterns of oppression are not only interrelated, but are bound together and influenced by the intersectional systems of society."[1] In other words, you can't discuss issues of gender without also considering race and ethnicity, class, and ability.

In spite of Jim Crow laws, or perhaps because of them, Southerners have always been forced to confront issues of race. We can't skirt around them or pretend they don't exist.

In his 2015 TED Talk, Rich Benjamin, author of the book *Searching for Whitopia: An Improbable Journey to the Heart of White America*, discussed the time he spent living in America's whitest communities doing research for his book. Benjamin traveled to suburbs in Utah, Idaho, and even New York. When he began to detail his time in Georgia the audience laughed, assuming that of all the places he traveled he was least accepted in the South. They were wrong. Benjamin explained that in Georgia he felt more comfortable there because he wasn't treated as exotic.[2]

As a Southerner, I'm no stranger to racist or homophobic attitudes, and I'm not ignorant of poverty or the conditions of the working poor. And thus, it is not difficult for the Southern feminist to realize that feminism cannot just be about gender but must also address race and ethnicity, sexual orientation, class, and even physical ability. Southern feminists know feminism must also address religion. The feminist movement must find a way to challenge churches that treat women like second-class citizens without chastising feminists for being women of faith in the first place.

On a lighter note, as a Southern feminist, I know better than to judge a woman for caring about fashion. I'm not going to look down on a stylish lady, shake my head, and cast her as a victim of the male gaze. I know that when it comes to fashion, it's not about getting the attention of men. It's not even just about clothes. Fashion is about confidence; it is a type of social communication.

As Birmingham–based style coach Megan LaRussa Chenoweth once said to me, "We as Southerners take pride in our heritage and ourselves and thus dress accordingly." Style is not about vanity. Good fashion is good manners. In the South, not dressing appropriately for an occasion is considered just plain rude!

As a Southern feminist, I understand the importance of Title IX and the attempt to stop sex discrimination in athletics. I live in a land where sport—especially football—is practically religion and not one reserved only for men. The average Southern woman will know just as much about sports as the average Southern man and will probably yell the loudest at an Alabama or Auburn game. So the idea that a woman shouldn't just be on the sidelines but also on the field is hardly a strange concept for me.

And finally, it is because of my Southern roots that I believe in sisterhood. No, I wasn't in a college sorority. I believe in sisterhood because I feel a kinship to nearly every woman and girl I meet, and I believe Southern hospitality has something to do with that. In the South, everyone feels familiar. We smile at strangers on the street and ask about their day. We invite you to come over for lemonade or sweet tea and actually mean it. And when we first meet you, we greet you not with a handshake but with a hug.

Since returning to my hometown of Birmingham in 2009 I've fallen head over heels for the South. In the past, I've often sought to prove to others that I am still a fervent feminist despite my Southern pride but now I've realized I'm a feminist because of it. And so, for me, Southern-fried feminism is the best kind.

Birmingham–You Don't Get to Hate It Unless You Love It

In her book *Writing Down the Bones*, Natalie Goldberg tells writers, "It is very important to go home if you want your work to be whole. You don't have to move in with your parents again and collect a weekly allowance, but you must claim where you come from and look deep into it. Come to honor and embrace it, or at the least, accept it."[1]

Ironically, it was leaving home that helped me accept, honor, and embrace where I'm from. I was born and raised in Birmingham, and like many of my peers, I couldn't wait to "get out." That's how we'd say it, as if our city were a cage. I'd complain about how boring and backward all of Alabama was and dream of the day I'd finally escape and move to New York.

Life—and a generous scholarship—instead took me to California where I attended UC Berkeley for graduate school. I fit in well in the West. I made friends fast, and in a lot of ways, I felt I'd finally found my people. Nevertheless, I was homesick. Obviously, I missed the family and friends I'd left back home, but it was more than that.

I missed how in the South you always feel as if you know the person next to you, even if you don't. So, you smile, nod, and strike up a conversation. It might begin as small talk about the weather—"It sure is hot out there today!"—but soon enough you're showing each other family photos or exchanging stories about your childhood. Sometimes you even share secrets and dreams. And if you're stranded on the side of the road, the kindness of strangers will rescue you long before AAA arrives. I missed grits, sweet tea, and Golden Flake Sweet Heat Barbecue potato chips. I even missed the rich red color of the earth.

Near the end of my first semester at Berkeley, I shared with a fellow student how much I was looking forward to going home for the holidays, and he asked, "Why would you want to go back to Birmingham, Alabama? There's nothing there but trees with strange fruit!" He then burst into laughter, so proud and amused with himself.

My rage left me speechless. I couldn't believe a young Black man would make a joke about the history of lynching in the South. But I felt something else at that moment that I wouldn't have words for until nearly twenty years later.

In the critically acclaimed film *The Last Black Man in San Francisco,* protagonist Jimmie Fails confronts someone who is idly putting down San Francisco with words that struck many reviewers of the movie: "You don't get to hate San Francisco. You don't get to hate it unless you love it."

The film's masterful treatment of themes such as gentrification and Black manhood had me fighting back tears when I saw the movie in theaters in the summer of 2019. And though the film hardly portrays San Francisco in a positive light, it made me miss the time I lived in the Bay Area too. But as soon as Fails said those words, the tears finally fell, and it wasn't San Francisco on my mind. It was Birmingham.

By then I had been back in my hometown for a decade. I had come to accept it, honor it, and embrace it. And I'd come to feel that you don't get to hate it unless you love it. Don't get me wrong, Birmingham is not an easy place to love, her hot humid breath choking me from May to September. Images of the foaming mouths of mad dogs and water hoses play in my mind on repeat like an emergency broadcast. But leaving Birmingham made me appreciate it in ways I couldn't as a kid—and when you love a place, you hate anything that hurts it.

I hate that more than fifty years after the end of Jim Crow, many of Birmingham's neighborhoods are still segregated. My diverse group of friends and I sometimes still turn heads when we go out for brunch–and it's not just because we're fine! I hate that many of our city's predominantly Black neighborhoods have been woefully underserved. I hate that some people don't feel safe in my city. And I hate that people still wield religion like a weapon, making my gay friends afraid to kiss or hold hands with their partners in public.

But when I returned to Birmingham in 2009, I began to love the city in ways I never thought I would. I saw that the city is bursting at the seams with artists and activists promoting unity and social change. And they're creating safe spaces for marginalized folks, redefining what Southern hospitality is all about. My city's civil rights legacy is a blueprint showing us how to challenge, change, or tear down the systems that continue to oppress people of color, women, and the LGBTQ+ community.

Joy is my resistance, and in Birmingham, I've learned to find that joy in the little things–in the city's great restaurants, kitschy shops, and wonderful parks. I've learned that teenage Javacia was wrong about Birmingham being boring. Most weekends there's so much going on that I have trouble deciding what to do.

I love Birmingham, and I will do what I can to prove it, whether that's by helping to raise money for local nonprofits or by telling the stories of our city's unsung heroes so others will get inspired to do their part too. I love Birmingham, and I will do what I can to make sure it is a city that loves me back.

A portion of this essay was originally published in the September 2019 issue of Birmingham magazine. Reprinted with permission.

Home Is Where Your Story Is

When people ask me where in Birmingham I grew up, I sometimes say "Everywhere." We moved around a lot, and the neighborhoods of Birmingham find their way into so much of what I write.

The Birmingham neighborhood of Ensley made me a poet. When I was one year old, my parents and I moved into a tiny apartment off Twentieth Street. I've written poems about playing kickball in the parking lot of that Ensley apartment complex and poems about the honeysuckle that grew on the fence to the rear of the lot. I've written about trips to see the candy lady and to the corner store.

After brief stints in College Hills and Titusville, my family settled in North Birmingham for several years. North Birmingham made me a storyteller. We moved into a big house just off Highway 31 that looked like the set of a horror movie. We were renting the house for next to nothing from a man who hadn't quite gotten around to fixing up the place but swore he would. He never did.

The high ceilings, peeling wallpaper, and chipped paint ignited my imagination. The larger-than-life cloudy mirrors that had been left behind by the previous tenants housed the spirits of people who'd died in the house, as did the stray cat that always hung around the front yard. I named her Miss Lucy, and she was the star of all my short stories.

I had to leave Birmingham to learn how to tell true stories in prose. After college in Tuscaloosa, Alabama, and graduate school in Berkeley, I moved to Louisville to be a newspaper reporter. My knack for writing personal essays landed me my own column and the chance to be included in a collection of feminist essays published by Seal Press.

Then I came home. When I moved back to Birmingham in 2009, I thought I was coming home to start a new career, leave journalism, and enter the classroom as a high school English teacher. But now I know I came home for the sake of my story.

In Birmingham, I get to share my story in local magazines and on my blog. I build my story through every friendship forged in this city of steel, sweat, and sweet tea.

In the preface of her bestselling memoir *Becoming*, former first lady Michelle Obama writes, "Your story is what you have, what you will always have. It is something to own."[1]

I now know that no matter where I live, my story will always be my home.

This essay was originally published in the March 2019 issue of Birmingham magazine. Reprinted with permission.

Having a Room to Write Is a State of Mind

In 2015, my writing group helped me buy a house.

Let me explain. No, the women of See Jane Write didn't put together a GoFundMe fundraiser to help my husband and me become homeowners. No, I didn't make the down payment on our house with an advance from a book deal or even with money saved from freelance writing gigs. But when you're the leader of a writing group for women, a group that's meant to encourage women to start that blog, write that book, or send that pitch, you have to practice what you preach—and not just in your writing life.

On December 31, 2014, I declared that 2015 would be the year I would go after all the things I once believed were beyond my reach. I made that declaration because I wanted to set a good example. I not only wanted to encourage women to write; I wanted to encourage women to live lives worth writing about.

Growing up, my family bounced from one rental home to the next, and I was convinced that to own a house you had to be rich, and you had to be white. As a Black girl from a low-income household, I was neither. Even though my parents worked very hard, they always struggled to make ends meet. They weren't able to purchase a house, and more than once we'd come home to find an eviction notice taped to the front door.

So when my husband came to me in February of 2015 and asked, "Do you want to try to buy a house?" a part of me wanted to burst into laughter. Another part wanted to run away from the conversation—literally. Being a homeowner terrified me because it seemed so unfathomable. But because of that promise I'd made to myself, I simply said, "Yes!"

Four months later we closed on our first house, and in June of 2015, we moved into our three-bedroom home. Long before the keys to the house were in our hands, I knew one of those bedrooms would be my new home office, my babe cave, my See Jane Write headquarters. Having a designated place to write was the thing I most looked forward to about moving into our new home.

Don't get me wrong, I love everything about my house. I love the way the hardwood floors feel beneath my bare feet. I love the high ceilings in the living room and the granite counter tops in the kitchen. But my home office is my sanctuary.

Virginia Woolf once said, "A woman must have … a room of her own if she is to write." Frankly, I've never needed a room of my own to write, but I longed for one anyway. As a girl, when I shared a room with my younger brother, I found a way to write my really bad poetry in spite of all the chaos that little brothers can bring. When I got married at twenty-five and was thus sharing my room again, my writing flourished, nonetheless. I could and would write anywhere. I could finish freelance articles at the dining room table, draft blog posts on the sofa, and type personal essays in bed.

I've come to realize that a room of one's own doesn't have to be a place with four walls and a door. The "room" can be the determination to write no matter what. The "room" can be your imagination that lets you temporarily escape this world and build worlds of your own.

If you are a woman with a story to tell, find your room—whether it's within or without—and just write. Write in spite of the chaos. Write because of the chaos. Write because you just can't help yourself.

This essay was originally published in the April 2019 issue of Birmingham *magazine. Reprinted with permission.*

My Mother's Daughter

The yellow socks almost break me.

It's February 26, 2020. My husband and I rise before dawn, and by the time we reach the hospital, it's still dark outside. I'm dressed in grey workout pants and a black graphic tee that reads, "She's an Andre 3000 verse in a world of mumble rap." Maybe I'm trying to remind my husband I am to be treasured in sickness and in health. Maybe I'm trying to remind myself.

I keep tugging on the black sweater draped over my T-shirt, wrapping it around my body like a mother swaddling her baby. I can't stop shaking, but I'm not sure if the shiver down my spine is from the cold air or fear. Next up—paper and plastic. Paperwork, paperwork, paperwork. Then a plastic wristband. It reads: *Bowser, Javacia H 39Y.*

"That's much too young for breast cancer," the nurses say. And I want to say, "Tell that to the tumor you're about to help the surgeon remove." But I just give them a half-smile. I rarely say what I'm thinking. I'm handed a plastic bag.

"Undress, place your clothes in here, and then put on the gown and socks on the bed."

I start to do as I'm told, but then I see those yellow socks. And suddenly my mind lifts my body from one hospital room to another, from my hospital room to my mother's. Too many moments with my mother have been spent in hospital rooms. Heart disease. High blood pressure. Stroke. Diabetes. Kidney failure. These are all in her medical chart and therefore in mine under family medical history.

Her most recent hospitalizations had been due to fits of violent vomiting that her doctors couldn't explain. Perhaps she'd gotten an infection through dialysis. Perhaps it was something else. One day, as I cleaned bile from her face and her hair, the yellow socks on her feet caught my eye and pissed me off.

Yellow is a tricky color. Bright yellow brings feelings of joy, hope, and new beginnings. It's the color of sunshine. But turn down the vibrance and a dull yellow looks unclean. It becomes the color of sickness. These socks were somewhere in between, and I needed them to pick a side, to tell me if I should have hope or not. Was I going to have more time with my mother? Was I going to have a chance to be a better daughter?

You see, on the outside, I'd been a good daughter—doing whatever she asked, speaking to her softly with love and respect, helping my father cover bills when needed. But on the inside, I would pity my mother. My narrow-minded view of the world made me wonder if all her illnesses had kept her from being the woman she was meant to be. Had sickness kept her from traveling the world, from having a career, from being more than a mother and a wife?

So when I see those yellow socks on my own hospital bed, I begin to wonder the same things about myself and wonder if my friends–once they learn about my diagnosis–will begin to pity me. The surgery is a success–if you can call getting a chunk of your boob cut out a triumph–and I'm home before noon.

***

At the time of my surgery, I had been told I wouldn't need chemotherapy, but by the beginning of May I'm sitting in a chair getting Adriamycin (a.k.a. the Red Devil) and Cyclophosphamide pumped through my veins. Next up, Taxol.

I go through five months of chemo that my oncologist and nurses say I "tolerated very well" because I didn't have to skip a session or be hospitalized. Through it all, I keep writing and working. I walk for exercise every single day.

During the day, I am Wonder Woman in a headwrap. At night–not so much. My thoughts are dark and twisty. I want to pray for a long life, but I can't. With the lasting side effects of chemo and the constant worry about recurrence, will life be worth living?

Despite my workaholic ways (when I was diagnosed, my first question to my doctor was "Will I still be able to work?"), I don't think about my work when I mull over my mortality in the middle of the night. I don't think about the book I haven't published, the magazines I haven't written for, or the awards I haven't won. I only think about how I want more time with my husband, my family, and my friends.

And that's when I realize that my mother has never needed my useless pity. No matter what illness she has faced, she has never let sickness steal her joy, and she has never let it keep her from doing what matters to her most–loving her children and her husband fiercely. When I told my brother that I'd been diagnosed with breast cancer one of the first things he said to me was that he knew this disease wouldn't beat me because "You come from Mama."

So I've decided that even if cancer kills me, it still won't win if I hold on to my joy until the very end. I come from Lesa. I am my mother's daughter.

How My Father Made Me a Feminist

My father, like many dads, declared himself the king of the grill long ago. My fondest memories are of hot summer days spent in my parents' backyard, listening to old school R&B while waiting for hot dogs and hamburgers to make their way off my dad's grill and onto my plate.

Growing up, I looked forward to certain holidays simply because I knew they meant my dad was going to fire up the grill. The fireworks on the Fourth of July were great, but not nearly as exciting as a backyard family barbecue. Sure, I appreciated the day off from school that Labor Day brought, but that was just a bonus to the barbecue and baked beans. And if we had an unseasonably warm winter, my dad would even grill out on Christmas Day—a gift just as good as anything under the tree.

But my father didn't just cook on red-letter days—he was just as comfortable in the kitchen at the stove as he was in the backyard at the grill. My father cooked most days of the year, as he was the parent in charge of dinner in our house. And while he was cooking, he was usually watching soap operas—*The Young and the Restless* is his favorite. In other words, my father, though a man most would call strong and tough, defied gender stereotypes in many ways.

My father made me a feminist, though I'm sure he'd never use this word to describe himself. But when I was a little girl, he made me feel that I was smart enough to do anything I could dream of. By doing most of the cooking for our family, he taught me, without saying a word, that gender roles are dumb. And he taught me that any man who treated me as any less than a queen wasn't worth my time. It took a few years for that lesson to sink in, but when I finally got it right and married my Mr. Right, it was an honor and a joy for my father to walk me down the aisle.

Ironically, my father is also why it took years for me to call myself a feminist. Ignorant of the true meaning of the word, teenage me would say things like, "I'll start calling myself a feminist when feminism stops being about hating men." Back then, I bought into the lie that feminism taught the message that all men are awful, and, as a bona fide daddy's girl, this was a message I clearly couldn't accept.

Eventually, I would discover that feminism isn't about hating men at all, but rather it's about equality. My father doesn't host backyard barbecues as often these days, but he still makes chicken, turkey, and his delectable dressing for Thanksgiving and Christmas. And no matter how old I get, I'll always be a daddy's girl.

If, like me, your parents are still living, count your blessings and spend time letting your parents know just how much you appreciate them. Remember to show gratitude for your chosen family too. No matter the season, share a meal with friends who are like family and family members you call friends, whether you're at a backyard barbecue, a beach bonfire, a kitchen table, or at a restaurant down the street. These moments could make you a better person. These moments could even make you a feminist.

This essay was originally published in the June 2019 issue of Birmingham magazine. Reprinted with permission.

My Brother and Me

When I told my brother I'd been diagnosed with breast cancer, he responded just as I knew he would: "Man, you got this. This shit ain't gonna beat you. Imma holla at God tonight, tell him to take care of my big sister, and you gonna be straight."

And that was that. I knew I would be fine because my baby brother said so. Even though I am seven years and six months older than my brother, even though I cooked his breakfast on the weekends, taught him how to tie his shoes, and helped him with homework, in some ways he has taken care of me as much as I've helped take care of him.

That care usually comes in the shape of three words: "Man, chill out." Those words have the power to stave off my panic attacks like no anxiety medicine ever could. But only when said by my brother. I'm not sure how two people so different could have been raised in the same home. And I'm not sure how two people so different could get along as well as we do.

If worrying were an Olympic sport, I'd be Michael Phelps. My brother on the other hand—nothing frazzles him. Not even a cancer diagnosis–and not because he trusts in the power of Western medicine. No, according to my brother, chemotherapy, radiation–that's all bullshit. That's why a few days after finding out I had cancer, he showed up at my house with a huge bottle of black seed oil and wouldn't leave until I drank some of it.

"It tastes like something you get at Auto Zone, but it works," my brother said. And he was right. Black seed oil tastes terrible, but every morning I take a shot of it, nonetheless. To be honest, I didn't add black seed oil to my supplement regimen because I believe it's a cure for cancer or anything else. I did it simply because my little brother asked me to.

A month after my diagnosis, I had a lumpectomy to remove the tumor in my left breast. The surgeon also removed a sentinel lymph node to test it for cancer, a process that required an injection of a substance that made my urine neon green. I knew my brother would get a kick out of this. I couldn't wait to tell him when he came over.

"You mean it's green like this!?" he asked, snatching up the bottle of Dawn dish washing liquid on the kitchen sink.

"Yep!" I said with a grin.

"Man, that's crazy!"

Of all the people who came by to visit me after my surgery, my brother was the only one I shared my neon green pee story with. He was also the only one who asked the one question I was eager to answer: "So when you gonna get back on your grind?" He wanted to know when I was going to get back to work, when I was going to get back to writing and building my business.

Everyone else kept urging me to rest, to take long naps, to lie on the sofa and watch Netflix. But my brother knew that the thing that would make me feel better, the thing that would make me feel like myself and truly help me heal would be working on my dreams. This is the one thing we have in common, our bond that is thicker than water and blood. We are dreamers.

Despite his cool, calm, collected attitude toward life, love, and everything in between, CJ is always on ten about his dream of being a famous music producer. And my brother is a dreamer and a doer. His music is not only used by emerging hip-hop artists but has been featured in commercials and popular TV shows too. His big dream is to get into film scoring. I am as confident that he'll achieve this goal as he is that I will beat cancer.

When we were kids, we had a secret handshake. Now we have our own hashtag #PowerToTheDreamers. We add it to the end of social media posts and with signatures in birthday cards.

The day after my surgery my brother called me Wonder Woman, but not in a way meant to pacify or patronize. He said it without pomp and circumstance as if it were my name or my job title. "I wore Wonder Woman underwear to the hospital," I told him, and we laughed.

My brother is the type of person who can know your flaws and faults, your worries and your weaknesses, who can see all of your anxiety and still also see your superpower.

Daughters of Eve

It's 2004, and I'm home in a room that was once my granny's den but is now my bedroom during breaks from grad school. My index finger and thumb pinch through the pages of the latest issue of *Elle* magazine. I skim an article about a nude performance art show in New York City, and it makes me remember the moment I first felt the grit of that city settle on my Southern skin. It felt like losing my virginity again, and I wondered if this was how Eve felt when she bit into the fruit that she'd been told would make her unclean.

My mother asks me to join her in the backyard to pick plums. With the sun baking our backs a richer shade of brown, we two brown women leap in the air to grab at the high limbs looking like kids on a basketball court with no ball who decide to see who has the best vertical to pass the time.

Mama wins.

She reminds me how to judge sweetness with a look and a squeeze. Once there were three of us. Granny loved plums. And I loved her. When people see old photographs of her and say I have her dimples, I don't bother with talk of my mother's adoption. I am certain I have her smile.

I don't remember much about my granny's brief bout with breast cancer. (Was it actually brief? Isn't that relative? I'm sure it didn't feel brief to her.) I don't even remember being sad or scared. Maybe because I didn't see her express either emotion. I just remember one day she had two boobs, and one day she didn't. And when she'd put on her fake boob, it meant company was coming over or we were going out.

A month before her death, when she got so sick that she couldn't keep her words straight, the doctors said, "The cancer is back, and it's spread." And for a moment I thought, "What cancer?"–until I remembered. I'm sure Granny never forgot. Yet she let it slip my mind because she never, ever talked about it. And because we don't share biology, I never had to share her medical history with my doctors. But nearly eighteen years after she left this earth, I will think of her breast cancer diagnosis when I receive my own. I will try to be like her. I will try to not be sad or scared. But I will fail.

I think about how I've decided already at the age of twenty-three that I don't want to be a mother. Not because I hate children or because I wasn't hugged enough as a child or because I'm selfish or any of the other ridiculous reasons people will hurl at me once I start making my decision known. I will go on to spend my twenties and thirties listening to countless people tell me that I will change my mind (which I don't) or that a woman's purpose is to birth children (which I'm sure it's not). I think of Granny and how she never gave birth to a child but was a mother and a grandmother, nonetheless. So I am certain even if I'm not a mother I can still leave a legacy.

But none of this has happened yet on this hot summer day in Granny's backyard. I look around and remember how much I loved this yard as a kid. Back then, it felt so big. My imagination would transform it into wild jungles and foreign lands. Now I stand here and feel I am a giant, but one who still has trouble reaching for what she wants.

Nostalgia gives me restless feet, and I want to sling off my Old Navy flip-flops and let the green grass tickle my toes as I did when I was a girl. But I don't. I know Mama wouldn't let me because she's just told me that last week while working together in the yard, she and Daddy unearthed a snake.

The mention of a snake makes me remember a poem about Eve I've been struggling to write for one of my classes, the poem I was supposed to be working on when I decided to read a magazine instead. The poem was part literature, part litigation trying to prove that Eve was framed, and it wasn't working. At all. Now I'm picking fruit from a tree. Maybe this should be a poem, I think, before shaking myself back into the moment. When you're a writer, words have a way of grounding you sometimes and at other times, they send you drifting away even when you're trying to stay put.

Staying in one place is hard for me. The year before this one I lived in three different time zones in twelve months–Alabama for a winter/spring internship, Kentucky for a summer internship, and California to start grad school in the fall. That year showed me I feel at home everywhere and nowhere.

Our arms grow weary from plum picking at the same time, even though my mom's arms were scrubbing the tub and toilet earlier that day. When she finished cleaning the bathroom, she came into my room and asked if she should hang the new shower curtain now or wait until Sunday–the day we were expecting guests for a backyard barbecue. I was tempted to say it didn't matter. But instead, I said, "Wait until Sunday," because it did matter and because I knew that's what I would do if I were the woman of the house.

"Woman of the house"–I turn that phrase over in my mind a few times and decide I like it better than "housewife," which my mom proudly calls herself now, her health too unpredictable for her to hold down a part-time job. But I decided long ago that "writer" and "career woman" were the titles I wanted to hold instead. Because of this, I often think my mother and I are complete opposites. But as we stand beneath this tree, she and I and Eve all seem the same. We are all women who want to bear fruit.

Writing Prompts:

Where are you from? Who do you come from? How has this shaped who you are?
What is home?
Write about someone you love and make the reader love them too.

Dear Alison,

We disagreed on a lot. You didn't understand my obsession with Beyoncé. You found it unhealthy, even unholy. And you preferred old-school hip-hop or Lecrae any day. You didn't like my advice to write from scars, not wounds. You said as Christians we were called to be more vulnerable than others. You'd sometimes remind me of obnoxious things I said to you when we were teenagers and make me wonder if I'd been a mean girl in shy girl's clothing.

What I'm trying to say is sometimes you made me doubt myself. But then you'd come right back and tell me that I inspired you. You said I inspired you to walk for exercise more. You said I inspired you to start a Facebook group for people with chronic illnesses and caretakers. Best of all, you said I inspired you to keep writing.

We wrote together often–once at Panera Bread, once at my favorite coffee shop, but mostly on Zoom calls. You were my friend, but you were also my See Jane Write sister. You joined the community for women writers that I founded in our hometown and stuck around even when global membership (and later a global pandemic) meant all meetups had to go virtual. You actually preferred this.

After I was diagnosed with breast cancer in January of 2020, we started texting more. You'd check on me to see how I was coping with chemo. I'd check to make sure you had gone to dialysis. Dialysis became something else our lives had in common back in 2016 when my mother's kidneys failed. During the summer of 2020, you would text me to check on my mom when she finally got a new kidney, even though you were still waiting for one of your own.

On September 2, you texted me to let me know you were having surgery the next day for a new port placement. "You will definitely be in my prayers," I said. And I meant it. With a port of my own bulging from the left side of my chest, I knew how important it was, what a relief it could be, to have a port that worked well.

"Thank you," you replied.

I had no idea that would be the last text I'd ever receive from you. We never got a chance to celebrate you getting a new kidney or me completing chemo. I never got the chance to go to a Lecrae concert with you. You never got a chance to finish your musical memoir on how Lecrae's music helped you battle depression.

But you did get the chance to start sharing your affirmations. You'd written a list of more than one hundred affirmations that you'd recite to yourself first thing in the morning and throughout the day. Months before your death you began sharing your affirmations in your Facebook group and on Instagram.

I deserve happiness.

I reject every thought that goes against God's Word.

I stand on my beliefs and values when trouble comes.

I am a good steward of my body, time, resources, and possessions.

I am healed in my body, soul, and emotions.

I delight myself in the Lord; therefore, I shall have the desires of my heart.

I am God's daughter.

Your cousin read some of your affirmations at your memorial service. The words were powerful, encouraging, and uplifting. At that moment, I felt that you were still with us. Because you wrote and shared your writing, you were able to comfort the friends and family mourning your death with your own words. This moment reminded me of the one thing that we could always agree on–language is legacy.

I miss you.

Girl Meets Blog

In 2008 I fell in love.

This isn't your typical "girl meets boy" kind of story. This is a story of "girl meets blog." In 2008 I started my first blog, and it was love at first post. I can't really explain it. I certainly wasn't new to writing—at the time I was working as a reporter for a weekly newspaper. I'd seen my byline on the pages of big-city papers like *The Seattle Times* and in national magazines. And I've called myself a writer since I wrote a really bad poem in second grade.

But something about blogging was different. Writing is like a sport in that you need to work at it constantly in order to get better. Blogging is my practice field. But it was also through blogging that I found my calling as a writer.

I first started blogging for the newspaper at which I worked at the time, but I loved blogging so much that in September of 2008 I launched a blog of my own. I called it GeorgiaMae.com, named for my late maternal grandmother, Georgia Mae Price.

On this site, I blogged about fashion, fitness, feminism, natural hair, pop culture, news, race issues, and so much more. Eventually, my husband started writing for my site too, publishing posts on urban music and relationships. My initial goal was for GeorgiaMae.com to be a feminist lifestyle site, but it eventually became a site about everything for everyone. And that was the problem.

My site lacked focus, and I had no ideal reader in mind when I produced content. That would be fine if I were just blogging as a hobby, but not if I wanted my site to be something more. I also learned I don't play well with others. Frankly, I didn't like sharing my blog with my husband. I believed that to truly reach my potential as a writer, I needed a room of my own, even if it was just a virtual one.

So on August 20, 2011, I started WriteousBabe.com, a place where I could think out loud, a place I could design with pretty pink accents and not worry about running off the men who dropped by to read my husband's musings on hip-hop. In part, Writeous Babe was meant to be a personal blog, a digital diary. But it was also a feminist lifestyle blog for women who write, chronicling my attempt to basically be the Black Carrie Bradshaw without the relationship drama and without leaving the South. I wanted to see my byline in my favorite magazines, write and publish books, land my own column on feminism, and have a fabulous wardrobe to boot.

My blog gave information and inspiration for women who write but also gave me a space to write about being a Black feminist, about being a married woman who is childless by choice, and about being a liberal who loves Jesus. With WriteousBabe.com, I fell in love with blogging all over again. My page views reached and then surpassed that of my other blog thanks to consistency and getting featured on a few major women's websites. I eventually let my husband have GeorgiaMae.com, which he rebranded as an urban music blog called Soul in Stereo.

The same year I started WriteousBabe.com, I also started See Jane Write. You see, when it comes to blogging, I am a true believer, preaching the power of digital writing with fervor. Soon people around town started emailing me or messaging me through social media whenever they had a question about writing or blogging. And paid writing gigs with local media outlets started to fall into my lap as editors heard about my work. Organizations began asking me to speak at their events.

As See Jane Write became more and more popular, I found myself blogging at WriteousBabe.com less and less. Instead, I was posting most of my content on the See Jane Write website because I realized See Jane Write was no longer just a women's writing group, and its website was no longer just a blog. See Jane Write had become a brand. See Jane Write had become a business, an award-winning business.

In 2012, the Women's Fund of Greater Birmingham presented me with their coveted SMART Award for innovation in business, philanthropy, and the arts. In 2017 The Write Life recognized See Jane Write as one of the best websites for writers (a recognition I would get in 2018, 2019, and 2021 as well). But these awards aren't why I fell in love with blogging.

I fell in love with blogging because it helped me find my platform. Both WriteousBabe.com and the blog I maintain for See Jane Write have been my space to write about faith, feminism, fitness, and so much more. Blogging has also helped me land opportunities to write on these topics for digital and print publications.

I fell in love with blogging because it helped me find my people. When I started See Jane Write, I had no idea that the women of this group would become my closest friends, but that's exactly what happened. We found one another through blogging, but in the process discovered we shared so much more.

I fell in love with blogging because it helped me find my purpose. Since I was a teenager, I've known that I wanted to use writing to empower women and girls. But with the ever-changing state of journalism and the publishing industry, I started to wonder what it would look like to actually live out that mission. Blogging became my way. Not only do I seek to uplift women with the stories I put out into the blogosphere, but I give women the knowledge and support they need to share their own stories too.

I'm in love with blogging, and blogging loves me back.

But as See Jane Write became more successful, I began to face the dilemma that so many writers wrestle with—how do I balance the business side and the creative side of writing? I was hosting workshops and events, creating e-courses and exclusive content for members, coaching women who wanted one-on-one help with their blogs or writing projects, doing speaking engagements, drafting e-mail newsletters, and planning strategic social media posts. I was juggling all of this with teaching full-time and freelancing for several different publications. When exactly was I supposed to find the time to wax poetic about feminism?

Nonetheless, I didn't close WriteousBabe.com. I still haven't. I probably never will. She's so special to me. Some people still refer to me as "The Writeous Babe."

Sometimes, I attempt to revive WriteousBabe.com, and each time I fail. All the self-help gurus and life coach types say that when you're struggling to be persistent, you should return to your why. In fact, this is exactly what I tell the women of See Jane Write when they're struggling to be consistent with writing and blogging.

I started WriteousBabe.com because I needed my own little piece of cyberspace. I needed a virtual "room of my own." I needed a space entirely my own where I could be free, where I could be myself, and where I could write myself whole again when needed.

Each time I return to blogging at WriteousBabe.com, it's for these same reasons. I return to my personal blog when I feel broken.

Blogging at SeeJaneWrite.net is for the sake of my business. Blogging at WriteousBabe.com is simply for the sake of my own well-being. But I am hopelessly unfaithful to myself. I haven't consistently updated my personal blog since See Jane Write blossomed into a business. But I miss spending time writing for my old blog because it feels like spending time with myself.

I know how much fun I can be. I am New Year's Eve parties that last until 5 a.m. I am Beyoncé concerts. I am superhero movies. I am brunch and bubbly wine. Sometimes I am even the blog post so good you just have to share it with your Facebook friends. But I am never my own number one girl.

I treat myself like the other woman, like a side piece, like that chick you call only when you're looking to have a good time or when you need your ego massaged. After the drinking or dancing is over, after "Self-Care Saturday" has come to a close, I tell myself I have to go. I promise I will call tomorrow even though I know I won't, even though I know I won't be back until I once again need to fall apart in my own arms. If I had a friend who was the side chick or the other woman of some man, I'd tell her to "Quit that fool!" But you can't quit yourself.

In 2016 I decided to start adding lifestyle content and personal posts to the See Jane Write blog since maintaining both sites proved to be so difficult. This has served me well, so far, as it's given me more of a creative outlet while also allowing readers to feel more connected to me and thus more connected to the See Jane Write brand. But there are still some things I can't bring myself to write about on a blog for my business, and there's still a part of me that flirts with the idea of bringing back the Babe.

Many of the content creators I have followed over the years have stopped blogging altogether. "Blogging is dead!" some folks proclaim. And I understand why many people feel this way. Many people would rather watch a video or listen to a podcast than read a blog post. To be honest, sometimes I'd rather watch a video or listen to a podcast!

Even if I one day ditch blogging for YouTube, I know the same keys to blogging success can help me with any other medium I choose to explore. Nail down your niche, create content with your audience in mind, be consistent, and be authentic. And most of all, tell your story. Tell your truth.

How to Be a Writer

I think I was in the fifth grade when I first declared I was going to be a writer when I grew up. That year I started reading the works of Maya Angelou. I decided I would one day be a famous poet like her. As I got older, the type of writing that I did changed, but my love for writing never did. Despite knowing I wanted to be a writer at the age of ten, I didn't feel like a real writer until nearly a decade later.

The first time I felt like a real writer, I was nineteen years old. I wrote a news story about an affordable housing initiative, pitched it to a newspaper in my hometown of Birmingham, and that paper published my article. I had my first clip and I felt legit.

But here's the thing. You don't need a book or a blog or a byline in a newspaper, magazine, or website to be a writer. To be a writer, all you have to do is write! Period.

This is why I tell the women in the See Jane Write community to write every day. Whether it's one page or even just one sentence–write every day. Whether that means getting up early or staying up late, write every day. Whether that means taking your journal with you to the bathroom, writing during your lunch break, or during your kid's nap time, write every day. Whether it's for five minutes or two hours, write every day.

You need to read a lot too. Stephen King once said, "If you don't have the time to read, you don't have the time (or the tools) to write. Simple as that." I read poetry and prose, fiction and nonfiction, and writing that blurs the lines of genre. Sometimes when I read, my skin tingles like the first time I saw fireworks. I can feel my heart hopscotch in my chest because I know that with each noun, verb, and even every article, I will be changed. I will be reborn and raised up by this village of vowels and consonants, then given the confidence to carry words of my own like a crown, unafraid to hoist hyperbole on my hip.

When I was a teacher, one of my coworkers told me that teaching isn't just a career, it's a lifestyle. And she was right. Standing before students in a classroom lecturing is just a fraction of what teachers do. Before and after official "work hours," we are writing lesson plans, grading papers, and worrying about students and sometimes even their parents. When you're a teacher, it bubbles over into almost everything else you do. Being a teacher affected what I wore, how I talked, what I would and would not post on social media, and even how I saw the world.

I've come to learn that writing is a lifestyle too. Seeing my byline in a newspaper or magazine didn't lead me to this revelation. I realized that writing is a lifestyle through my journaling practice.

I journal A LOT. Sometimes, my journaling looks a lot like it did when I was a teenage girl. I simply write about what I've done that day or the day before. Sometimes I write about lessons I've learned. Sometimes my journal entries are prayers. Sometimes I simply jot down ideas. But most times I journal to write my future into existence. I write about the life of my dreams as if it's already my reality. I write about the goals I want to accomplish as if I already have.

Zora Neale Hurston once wrote, "There are years that ask questions and years that answer." No matter the year, I use writing to do both. *Did God give me cancer? Can a Black woman be a feminist? Can a feminist be a wife?* These are just a few of the questions I've tackled through writing. I use writing to figure out what I don't know and what I do, what I think and why I think it, how I feel and what I should do about it.

I should confess to you that I talk to myself often, and I'm convinced this is because I'm a writer too. Do all writers talk to themselves? Are our brains so full of words that our fingers can't get them out fast enough, so they start spilling from our lips?

I've been talking to myself since I was a child. My parents assumed I was chatting with an imaginary friend. My granny thought I was praying. My atheist friends would make a joke here. They would say that God is an imaginary friend or that talking to yourself and praying are the same thing. Sometimes I wonder if they're right–about the last one at least–but not because I question God's existence. It's just that sometimes I think that the best place to find God is within myself. And I do that through writing too.

When writing is your lifestyle, you may also want it to be how you make a living. And I am not here for the starving artist cliché. I want to be a well-fed writer, and I want you to be one too.

I was in high school when I finally asked someone how I could make money as a writer and that person told me I could be a journalist. And so that's what I decided I would be. Today, however, there are so many ways to make money as a writer.

FREELANCE JOURNALISM

After finishing college and grad school, I worked as a staff reporter at *The Courier-Journal* in Louisville. But today, I earn most of my income as a freelance journalist. I write for print and digital publications and for local, regional, and national media outlets.

You don't need to quit your job and go to journalism school to become a freelancer. I have two degrees in journalism, and nobody cares. No editor I've worked for as a freelancer has ever asked about my educational background. They just want to know if you can do the work. So show them that you can by posting reported pieces on your blog or guest blogging for a site you love to read.

Having good story ideas and knowing how to pitch them well will obviously help boost your freelance writing career. But to be honest, my secret to success has been building buzz and cultivating community. Most of the freelance writing gigs I've gotten have been through relationships with editors and other writers or because someone found me through my blog or social media. So if you decide to be a freelance journalist, don't keep it to yourself!

BOOKS

Most writers want to make money by publishing books. You can do this by working hard to land an agent and a book deal, or you can self-publish. Either way, if you want to really make some money, you have to market your work. People can't buy your book if they don't know it exists. Let's hope I make some money from this book you're reading right now!

COPYWRITING AND EDITING

Another way you can make money with your writing talent and skills is to help other people's work sound better. You could be a ghostwriter or coauthor for someone who has a great story to share but is having trouble sharing it. Or you could edit other people's writing. You could write newsletters or blog posts for companies or organizations.

If you want to do this, be sure to nail down your niche. While you may think it's a good idea to market yourself as someone who can write anything for anyone, you're more likely to get gigs if you specialize in something and can position yourself as an expert. If you're the one who helps all your friends make smart money moves, perhaps you could be a personal finance writer.

I must confess that I don't exactly follow the "nail down your niche" rule because my niche is broad AF. What's my niche? Women! If I had to narrow it down a bit, I'd say I write women's lifestyle content or maybe I'd say I focus on "wealth and wellness" because I write a lot of personal finance and health and fitness content. But really what I do is this: I write stories for women and about women and help women write stories of their own. That's it. That's the tweet. (No, really, that's actually my Twitter bio.)

BLOGGING

Along with getting paid to write blog posts for companies or organizations, you can also get paid for content you create on your own blog through affiliate links and sponsored posts. I mostly see my blog as a form of content marketing. It's my way of promoting myself. And it's helped me land freelance writing gigs, speaking engagements, and more.

E-COURSES AND SUBSCRIPTION SERVICES

After seeing other bloggers do it, I realized that I could take the informational and inspirational content of my blog, expand on it and package it into an e-course that I could sell to my readers and others. The ideas for my e-courses always come from my readers. There are always certain questions that people ask me again and again. So I create courses to answer these questions. You can easily do the same.

If you have enough people who want help over a long period of time, you could also start a membership site or subscription service. I've done this through See Jane Write. Members get access to exclusive content to help them with writing, blogging, or brand building.

SPEAKING ENGAGEMENTS AND EVENTS

When I started See Jane Write, I started hosting quarterly events to help women with writing and blogging. See Jane Write wasn't a business at that time. I didn't charge for the events, and I paid for everything with my own money (much to my frugal husband's chagrin). At this point See Jane Write was just a VERY expensive hobby.

But because of the buzz I was building, people started asking me to come to speak at their events. At first, I was doing this for free, too, but then one day someone asked my speaker fee, and I realized I could actually be getting paid for this. And thus, I discovered another way that writers could make money—speaking engagements. Don't be afraid to share your story or your expertise with others through in-person or virtual presentations.

Eventually, I started charging for events too. Though it is very difficult to make a profit from events (ticket sales usually just barely cover the expenses for throwing an event), it is possible if you get enough sponsors.

COACHING

I sometimes call myself an accidental entrepreneur. When I started See Jane Write, it was meant to be simply a small group of women getting together once a month to talk about the writing life. But people started asking for events, and so I gave them events. And then people started asking for one-on-one help, and I gave them that too. At first, I gave them that one-on-one help for free. I was running all over town after a long day of teaching, meeting people at their favorite coffee shop and helping them outline their book, launch a blog, or jumpstart a freelance writing career. I was getting paid a smoothie and smile.

Finally, a business coach made me realize that what I was doing was called consulting or coaching and that I should be getting paid for it. So I started a formal coaching program, and this has been my most lucrative venture yet. I love seeing my clients write and publish books, launch blogs, start businesses, and see their bylines in their favorite publications.

So if you have several people regularly emailing you asking if they can "pick your brain" on a topic, you may have a coaching practice in the making. Do a few sessions for free in exchange for testimonials once they have results. Then launch your coaching business and use those testimonials on your website and promotional material.

A word of caution: don't feel pressured to pursue every possible source of income mentioned here, especially if you don't have a pressing financial need forcing you to do so. In fact, it's probably best to just focus on getting really good at one or two.

As the saying goes, "You can do anything, but not everything." Or if you are determined to do it all – don't try to do it all at once.

How to Be a Goal Digger

As with any relationship, money complicates things. As I've said, to be a writer, all you have to do is write. To be a writer who makes money, you have to figure out how to be both an artist and an entrepreneur.

Back in 2017, I took a solo weekend writing retreat to start writing a book (that would eventually become the one you're holding in your hands). But I spent several hours on the first evening of my retreat wrestling with my muse like Jacob tussling with an angel. I picked up my phone to tweet 140 characters or less, lamenting the irony of having writer's block when I was on a writing vacation. Then I realized that lack of inspiration was hardly my problem. I realized I had too many ideas, too many thoughts, and I couldn't pluck any prose from all that noise.

No, I hadn't gone on my writing retreat empty-handed. I had a complete outline saved in my Google Drive. But I had another outline for another book scribbled in one of my journals. And I simply couldn't choose.

So I took a break to listen to a podcast about navigating the intersection of art and entrepreneurship. I realized this was causing the Royal Rumble going on in my head. One book idea felt like art. The other book idea felt like a smart business move. In frustration, I exclaimed to the air in my hotel suite that I wished I could live a life in which I could do nothing but write and never worry about business or branding or marketing.

But this was a lie. This kind of life would be hell for me because I'm an extrovert. I'm so much of an extrovert that I spent the final night of my solo writing retreat sitting at the hotel bar chatting with the bartender for hours because I missed humans!

I don't want to sit home all day, every day behind my laptop lost in thought. I love being around other people. I love networking. I love brainstorming email and social media marketing strategies. I love the business side of writing. But for so long I've felt guilty for that. For so long, I've felt that this made me less of a writer, less of an artist. But I've finally realized this isn't true.

Just as women wear many different hats–wife, mother, auntie, boss, sister, daughter, friend–writers can do the same. Some days we need to wear our artist hat and get in a quiet space to create. Other days we need to put on our entrepreneur hats so we can market our masterpieces.

But you must decide what you want your days to look like. You need to set some goals to go after. What's your vision for your life? Write the vision and make it plain!

Describe what you want your life to look like five or so years from now. Consider every facet of your life–not just your writing career. Think about your relationships, your health and wellness, your home, your spirituality, your community service, and even what you want to do for fun. If this overwhelms you, start by simply describing your ideal day.

Armed with your vision, you can then set specific and measurable goals for yourself. Once you're clear on what you want, you need to figure out how you're going to get it. You know how the saying goes—a goal without a plan is just a wish. Break down your goals into smaller tasks, and plan when you will work on each task. Give yourself deadlines.

Along the way, you're going to need encouragement and support from like-minded women. That's why community is so important. Your vision can help keep you motivated too. Make a vision board and hang it someplace where you'll see it often.

Next, you need to develop a writing regimen and start setting aside time to work on your goals. If you are a blogger, try taking blog dates, as I like to call them, and batch produce content. A blog date is when you take your laptop to your favorite library or coffee shop and work on blog content for hours. You can do this at home if you have to, but I find that it's best that I get out of the house, so I'm not distracted by laundry, dishes, or *Law & Order* reruns. Be sure to go on these blog dates with a plan. Otherwise, you'll waste time staring at a blinking cursor on a blank screen and binging on coffeeshop pastries.

I plan out my blog content a month in advance, and I try to create the content a week in advance. Blogging can be broken down into three steps: produce, polish, promote. You must write your posts, edit and format your posts, and then create and schedule social media posts to promote your content. If you want to publish a new post each week, you could batch produce content for the month one weekend a month during a blog date or two. If that's not feasible, here's another schedule you could consider:

Tuesday: Outline your post
Wednesday: Write your post
Thursday: Edit your post
Friday: Work on images and social media promos for your post
Monday: Publish your post and schedule promotions

If freelance writing is part of your vision, but you're still working your day job, be sure not to bite off more than you can chew. That quote "I'd rather choke on greatness than nibble on mediocrity" sounds cute and all until you literally can't breathe because you're having a stress-induced panic attack. Be realistic about how many stories you can handle each month and stick to that!

To determine how many stories you can do each month, you need to break down your story production process into steps and figure out how much time you need for each step. My process includes researching, reporting, transcribing, outlining, writing, and editing. Back when I was still teaching, I could do one step per day, which meant I could do one reported piece per week.

If you're working on a book, I recommend giving yourself daily assignments. This assignment could be to write five or ten pages each day or to write for thirty minutes or one hour a day. If you're writing a collection of essays, perhaps you can write one essay a day.

Now you may be thinking, "But I don't have time to write. I'm just too busy." Stop it. Everyone is busy. Your busy schedule doesn't make you special. Sorry. And let's be honest, we make time for the things we want to do. So if you want to be a writer, make time to write. Commit to devoting at least five hours a week to working on your writing goals. Schedule this time and treat it like an appointment that you can't miss. (Side note: This doesn't apply to you if you are caring for a newborn or adjusting to some other major life change. You, my friend, are too busy.)

Being a writer who makes an income, and an impact, means building a platform–especially if you're interested in writing nonfiction such as memoir or essays or if you're planning to self-publish. *If I write it, they will come.* If this has been your motto for marketing your work, you need to stop lying to yourself. You must market your work–for real. People can't read your writing if they don't know it exists.

So many of the women writers I work with struggle with the idea of self-promotion. They believe that marketing their work is the same as bragging about their talent. But as the late, great Muhammad Ali once said, "It's not bragging if you can back it up!"

Know your value. Know what your work adds to your readers. Instead of feeling guilty for telling someone to read your articles, books, or blog posts, you should feel guilty if you *don't* share them! Think about it, if you have written something that is going to educate, motivate, empower, inspire, or even entertain someone, why would you not share it? Why are you keeping this valuable work from the people who want and need it?

Perhaps you have no qualms about promoting your work, but you just don't know how. Here are some of the many ways to promote your writing:

EMAIL

Start an email list using a service like Mailchimp, ConvertKit, Flodesk, or Constant Contact. Embed sign-up forms on your website in prominent areas such as the header, the sidebar, and/or within blog posts. You could also add a pop-up sign-up form.

Give readers a reason to sign up for your email list. Let them know what kind of special content you'll be sending to their inboxes and offer an opt-in incentive. Also known as a lead magnet, the opt-in incentive should be free content you give in exchange for the email address. This content should solve a problem faced by your ideal reader. For example, many of the women who read my blog want to get serious about writing, but they're not sure where to start. So one of my opt-in incentives is a free mini-course called Seven Ways to Jumpstart Your Writing Career.

Share valuable information with your email list often and promote your products or services to this list occasionally. Every email shouldn't be asking your list to buy your book. A good rule to follow is give, give, give, ask.

SOCIAL MEDIA

Some people say you need to be on all social media platforms all the time. While this would be great, so would a world of unicorns and cupcakes trees. Most people simply can't do this. My recommendation is to pick one or two platforms that you enjoy and that your ideal reader frequents and focus on those. And be consistent!

Remember it's called social media for a reason. Don't simply use it to promote your work. Use social media to spark conversations and connect with other writers too.

GETTING FEATURED

Pitch yourself to be interviewed on podcasts or to do a guest post on your favorite blog. Traditional media such as newspapers, magazines, TV, and radio can still be great sources of promotion too. Reach out to the editors and producers in charge of planning content and request coverage. (Pro tip: Don't approach media outlets saying they should feature you on their show or in their publication because you're so dope. Focus on the value you can offer their audience.)

NETWORKING

Attend in-person or virtual networking events that will attract your ideal reader. Join a local writing community. Attend conferences that give you a chance to meet agents and editors.

SPEAKING ENGAGEMENTS

Now that you're feeling froggy, why not try to land some speaking engagements? You can speak on topics related to your book or blog or your niche as a freelancer. And you can promote your brand or blog or sell your books at the event.

LIVE EVENTS

If you can't land an opportunity to speak at a conference or to a local organization or company, create an opportunity of your own by hosting a live event. If you don't want to host in-person events, you could always host virtual events such as webinars. You could also just host a networking event centered on the theme of your brand, book, or blog.

Your Ideal Reader

A few times now, I've mentioned your "ideal reader," and you may be wondering who that is. Your ideal reader is someone who is not just a follower but also a fan. Your ideal reader is that person (who's not your mom or favorite aunt) who not only reads your work but shares it with others. Your ideal reader is that person who promotes you and all you do better and more frequently than you promote yourself.

If you don't yet have a specific person in mind for your ideal reader, look inside for help. Think of the person you used to be before you grew, evolved, and transformed into the person you are today. That's the kind of person who would benefit most from the stories and information you have to share.

For example, let's say you are a body-positive fashion and fitness blogger striving to help plus-size women feel confident, stylish, and chic, as well as healthy. Think about the person you were before you felt the confidence you now enjoy. Think back to when you hated everything in your closet and had no idea how to put items together to create flattering and fashionable looks. Think back to when you wouldn't try yoga or running because some idiot told you that you had to be skinny to do so. Think back to when you longed to feel good about your wardrobe and yourself. That person that you were back then, that's your ideal reader. When you're promoting your work, go where your ideal reader would be.

OK, that's a lot. I know. So take a breath and remember this—writing is a lifestyle, but don't make writing your entire life. Toni Morrison once said, "You are not the work you do; you are the person you are."

This can be hard to accept—especially for writers. For years, I declared that writing isn't just what I do—it's who I am. But this mindset can cause us to tie our self-worth to our work, which can either cause us to work too much—or not work at all. Let me explain.

I once asked the women on my email list to share with me the biggest obstacle they were facing as they were trying to go after their writing goals. The overwhelming answer was FEAR, specifically the fear of rejection. I think a lot of this fear comes from seeing the rejection of your work as a rejection of you as a person. But when you feel whole and complete outside of your work, you can handle rejection. You can keep facing the no until you hear a yes. Or, better yet, you can stop asking for a seat and build your own table.

Writing Prompts:

Write about one of your biggest writing goals as if you have already achieved it.
Write a letter to your ideal reader.

Write Like a Girl

On my eleventh birthday, I declared I was a woman. I have no idea why. My budding boobs barely filled my training bra, and I wouldn't get my period for another year. But it was as if turning eleven declared I was number one and said it again for good measure, and I believed it.

I can't recall exactly what I decided to wear on this special day, but I do remember slouch socks were involved. I also remember that I didn't want a party because birthday parties were for children. A woman–especially one who at the time fancied herself a poet–should spend her birthday having a quiet evening at home writing in her journal, reflecting on her past, and making plans for the years to come.

What I'm trying to say is eleven-year-old me was ridiculous. But I think about this girl often. Sometimes to become the woman you're meant to be, you must remember the girl you used to be. Sometimes you must write like a girl.

When you write for a living, it can be hard to remember how to do this. When you write for a living, you can easily forget to write for yourself. You can forget to write simply for the love of words, for the joy of stringing together sentences. It can be hard to remember what it felt like to write with no regard for readers or a deadline, but that's what writing like a girl is all about. To write like a girl is to wake up early–even on your birthday—or stay up late–even on a school night—to scribble personal prose in your favorite notebook while sprawled across your bed, hair piled into a messy bun because you don't want any distractions, not even the curls you twirl around your finger when you're in deep thought. To write like a girl is to write because you just can't help yourself.

Writing like a girl is the craft of writing in its purest form. Sometimes I think back to that eleven-year-old girl–who thought she was a woman–and I challenge myself–just for a few moments–to forget about building a brand or pitching publications and just write. Yes, I can get back to business later, but right now, just write.

The yoke is easy. The burden is light. Just write.

How to Make Lemonade

Inspired by Beyoncé's *Lemonade*

You know how the saying goes, "When life hands you lemons, make lemonade." But 2020 didn't hand me lemons. The lemons came raining down upon me:

Breast cancer diagnosis.
Lumpectomy.
Global pandemic.
Constant reminders of racism.
Civil unrest.
Chemotherapy.
The death of a close friend.
Radiation.

I initially wanted to title my blog post announcing my diagnosis: "Y'all Thought I Was Inspiring Before—Hold My Boob!" Fortunately, I decided against that, but that tentative title explains a lot.

"Inspiring" is a word that people have used to describe me for years thanks to the stories and encouraging messages I share on my blog and on social media. But what a lot of people don't realize is that when I post inspirational quotes on Instagram or share stories about the importance of believing in your dreams and not giving up, I'm talking to myself and letting others eavesdrop on the conversation. I think about quitting every single thing I do every single day, and this was never truer than when I was going through cancer treatment. When you're facing cancer, you spend your days vacillating between fearing death and praying for it.

Chemotherapy brings more lemons than hair loss. Nausea. Fatigue. Irregular heartbeat. Low white blood cell count. Low red blood cell count. Neuropathy. Hand-foot syndrome. Mental fog (a.k.a. chemo brain).

Though people told me radiation is just like "a little sunburn," it was no day at the beach. At first, I was fine. But then the treatment started to make me feel utterly exhausted, and the discomfort from the radiation burns made sleeping nearly impossible. For about a week, the burns were so painful I couldn't lift my left arm without crying out in agony. But through it all, I kept sharing my story.

And on the days when I wanted to give up, I shared even more and added some humor for good measure.

This wasn't without its drawbacks. Some folks saw my posts and assumed I was unfazed by cancer or cancer treatments and therefore free to do whatever favor they'd been waiting to ask me for. So I also made it known that if anyone were to ask me to do anything I didn't want to do, I would play the cancer card. No, really. I actually bought a laminated card labeled "The Cancer Card" and posted a pic of myself holding it.

But I've come to believe that sometimes God allows us to face dark times so we can later be a light to others. I've been able to use my breast cancer experience to be a support system and a sounding board for others battling this disease. Don't get me wrong. This revelation doesn't make hardships easier to accept. I would rather we all just not have cancer in the first place. Cancer is stupid. Chemo sucks. And radiation is a pain–literally. But being able to help others shows me my suffering was not in vain. It motivates me to heal and live my best life so I can inspire other cancer survivors to do the same.

Iyanla Vanzant once said, "When you stand and share your story in an empowering way, your story will heal you and your story will heal somebody else." So the stories I've shared weren't just to inspire the people who read them. The stories gave me a sense of purpose and helped me make sense of a disease that doesn't make sense at all.

So how do you make lemonade? You start with eight lemons, no matter their shape. They could be shaped like a broken heart or like the tumor growing inside your left breast. Take each lemon and squeeze as hard as life sometimes squeezes you. Add a half-pound of sugar–the sweetness of your smile and your laugh. It cuts the tartness of turmoil. Add the zest of a half lemon–a bit of humor, a dash of comic relief.

You'll need a pint of water. Mix it all together. Pour the water from one jug then into another several times. Strain it all through a clean napkin. They need a filter. They can't take this at full strength. The flavor is too much, it puckers the mouth and locks the jaw. Let it chill before you serve. Then let them drink, let them taste your story–your pain—and call it refreshing. Believe it or not, it will refresh you too. Sometimes. But be careful to never let them drink you dry.

Writing Prompt:

When life gives you lemons, how do you make lemonade? How do you make the best of bad situations?

The New New Year's Eve

It's December 31, 2020, New Year's Eve, my favorite holiday.

Believe it or not, New Year's Eve has been my favorite holiday since I was a kid. Each year my parents, little brother, and I would stay up late eating junk food, drinking Kool-Aid, and watching Dick Clark's *New Year's Rockin' Eve*. We'd count down from ten and when the clock struck midnight, we'd yell "Happy New Year!" as loud as we could as if we hoped God would hear and decide to make this trip around the sun different. We hoped this would be the year we had enough money to pay every bill, every month.

Once I was old enough to spend New Year's Eve at dance clubs with a glass of cheap champagne in my hand, I would still call my parents and my brother just after midnight even if it meant hunkering down in a dirty bathroom stall so I could hear their voices. No boom of bass was loud enough to drown out the sounds of home.

This New Year's Eve looks different. I look different. I've slipped a little black dress on my body that's twenty pounds lighter than it was in January. I've slicked berry-colored lipstick on my mouth. I've blended bronze eyeshadow on my lids. And I have joyfully, gleefully, painted mascara onto my eyelashes–eyelashes that I didn't have two months ago.

Two months ago, I didn't have eyebrows either. I didn't have hair on my head, my legs, or my arms because just three months ago I finished five months of chemotherapy to treat the stage two breast cancer I was diagnosed with at the start of the year. Last New Year's Eve, my curls nearly reached my waist. This year I have only an inch of hair, but after sporting headwraps for seven months, I'm eager to show off my coif.

Unfortunately, I'm all dressed up with nowhere to go. While I was coping with one Big C, the world was dealing with another–COVID. Back in March when businesses started to close their doors and government officials told us to stay "safe at home," we all thought we'd be quarantined for just a couple of weeks. Nine months later, my husband and I still don't feel safe going to the movies or out to eat.

So we're celebrating New Year's Eve at home. For my husband, Edward, December 31 is just another day on the calendar. But because it's my favorite day of the year, he always plays along. He's put on a suit and a button-down shirt and completed the look with a blue pocket square that, when looking at pictures from the evening, we notice matches my nail color.

Yes, we take pictures. We get dressed up to stay home. We get dressed up to play board games and eat Rotel dip while sitting on our couch. But first, we take pictures for the obligatory New Year's Eve Instagram post. This year's post feels different. This year's post feels like a victory, a triumph, and a declaration.

I believe in the magic of New Year's Eve. I believe New Year's Eve should be spent with friends who are like family and with family members who are also friends. I believe in making silent wishes during the final countdown. I believe in kissing at midnight. I believe in champagne toasts even though I don't really like champagne.

I believe every New Year should begin with brunch. I believe one must wear a paper Happy New Year tiara to said brunch without irony and without shame. I believe a new planner magically gives me the power to make all of my dreams come true.

Cancer didn't change this. Chemo couldn't kill this. And while COVID has made my NYE celebration a party of two, and means I'll have to make my own brunch, the pandemic won't stop me either. This year tried to kill me. For real. There's no hyperbole in that statement. But here we are. It's December 31, 2020, and I'm still here.

On this New Year's Eve—which is still my favorite holiday in spite of everything—these words from my favorite Lucille Clifton poem, "won't you celebrate with me,"[1] have never meant as much to me as they do now:

come celebrate
with me that everyday
something has tried to kill me
and has failed.

What My Summer Bucket List Taught Me about Life after Cancer

It's May 29, 2021–Memorial Day Weekend and the unofficial start of summer— and I'm standing in my closet trying to figure out what to wear to a rooftop birthday brunch that my husband and I have been invited to. Thanks to COVID and cancer, it will be my first time gathering with a group of friends since early March of 2020. My closet gives this away. There's dust on my clutches and most of my shoes. There's been no need for cute sandals, and the only bags I've used are those big enough to carry all the things a girl needs to tote to chemo.

But now the coronavirus vaccine is helping things go "back to normal" slowly but surely. For me, however, going "back to normal" is no longer an option.

I'm glad that's all behind you now. People say this to you often after you've finished active cancer treatment. No more surgeries. No more chemotherapy. No more radiation. Slash. Poison. Burn. Done. They think you should be all better now.

On social media, you share the victories–the videos of you ringing the bell after completing treatment. The picture of you enjoying tacos after the nausea's gone and your taste buds come back. Your first post-chemo selfie with hair.

But what they don't see is the fear. They don't see that every time you lift food toward your mouth, you wonder if something in it could cause cancer. They don't see that anytime absolutely anything on your body aches, you think it's a sign of recurrence. They don't know that the scents of spring and summer remind you of chemo and send your emotions spiraling down, down to deep dark places. They don't know that you think about cancer every single day.

"Are you afraid of death?" my therapist asks me.

"No, I'm afraid of cancer making life feel like it's not worth living," I reply.

In early May, the lymph nodes in my neck are swollen, I feel a sharp pain in my left breast, and I notice a pimple on my right breast. Dr. Google and I decide I now have inflammatory breast cancer or lymphoma or both, and I give myself twelve months to live.

The swelling subsides, the pain eases and the pimple disappears, but I keep the appointment I've made with my oncologist. She explains to me what inflammatory breast cancer actually looks like, that those swollen lymph nodes were probably from a sinus infection, and that the sharp pain in my left breast is being caused by nerve endings coming back to life. What I thought was a sign of more disease was actually a sign of healing.

"The kind of breast cancer you had is very curable," my oncologist reminds me.

Slash, poison, burn, and pop a pill called Tamoxifen every day for the next ten years. That's my treatment plan. I take it seriously. Every day at 10 a.m., an alarm sounds on my phone reminding me to "Take your meds or die." (My oncologist keeps trying to get me to change that to "Take your meds and live" or "Take your meds, please," but I've always been a tough love kind of girl.)

I also decided to cut back on meat, dairy, and sugar. I buy organic as much as my budget will allow. I stopped drinking alcohol. And I no longer use deodorant with aluminum salts. Yet, nothing feels like enough.

"You're doing everything you can to prevent a recurrence," my oncologist assures me. But for shits and giggles, she plays worst-case scenario with me (something my therapist often does, and now I'm wondering if they've been conspiring). "Let's say in five years the cancer does come back," she says. "That will then be the time to worry about it. Now is the time to live it up!" Her words remind me of something my husband said to me: "You're wasting your victory lap worrying about what may or may not happen."

I take out the pink journal that I bring with me to every appointment and check-up, and I write: "Doctor's Orders: LIVE IT UP!" And I decide that I will "live it up" by becoming obsessed with self-care. Not the commercialized self-care that says you need to buy this and that to fix yourself. Self-care for me is eating five servings of fruits and vegetables every day but also eating the occasional slice of pie and not feeling guilty about it. Self-care is getting enough exercise and getting enough rest. Yes, self-care is bubble baths and massages and painting my nails. But it's also praying, reading, and writing. Self-care is an easy morning spent sipping a cup of green tea.

My husband and I go to the birthday brunch. I'm relieved to find I haven't forgotten how to talk to humans who aren't performing medical procedures on me. And I want more. I realize self-care is also spending time with the people I love. After the brunch, I spend the rest of the afternoon with my cousins and my favorite aunt (because you know all Black folks have a favorite auntie).

When I get home, I decide to write a bucket list for summer 2021. The first draft of my summer bucket list looks like a directory of local restaurants. You can probably relate. In summer 2020, we couldn't visit any of our favorite eateries because COVID forced many establishments to close their dining rooms. But that wasn't the only thing that kept me from my favorite local haunts. In summer 2020, for me, most food tasted like metal or sand or made me sick to my stomach.

The second draft of my summer bucket list looks like a TBR log, a litany of literature. Quarantine probably reminded you how much you love getting lost in a good book. And summer 2020 I used novels and nonfiction to escape the hum and the beeps of the chemo machines.

The next draft of my summer bucket list looks like a guest list as I write down the names of all the people I haven't hugged in over a year. You probably had your own friends and family tour in summer 2021. But in summer 2020, I often wondered not *when* I'd see my loved ones again but *if* I'd see them again.

Breast cancer changed everything, so for me, there will be no going back to normal. But as I was working on my bucket list, I realized that maybe that's OK. A bucket list is supposed to be a list of things you want to do before you kick the bucket. Cancer forces you to take the bucket list back to its roots and ask yourself, "What would I do if this summer were my last?"

Even after your surgeon cuts the tumor from your body, even after your last dose of chemo and final round of radiation, cancer still sits on your shoulder, whispering in your ear, reminding you that life as you know it can end in an instant. You learn to take nothing and no one for granted.

I decide to write some summer declarations in my journal:

I will drive hundreds of miles to hug my friends and fly across the country so I can hold my niece for the first time. I will see my parents' faces without a mask, and they will see mine.

This summer I won't sweat the small stuff, but I will appreciate the little things. I don't need trips to exotic lands. I just want to go to the movies! I will enjoy my summer reads without chemo fog clouding my brain.

After a summer with a constantly queasy belly and no taste buds, I will savor brunch and tacos and the occasional scoop of ice cream, and I will not count a single calorie. I will try that fitness class I keep seeing on Instagram–not to lose weight but because I'm glad to have the energy to move.

I will wear dresses with spaghetti straps and let the world see the battle scars that cancer and chemo left behind because I won. I will go to the beach with my husband, slip on a swimsuit, and not chastise my body for belly bulge or thighs that jiggle. I will honor it for staying alive against the odds.

While I wouldn't wish cancer on anyone, I do wish everyone could have something that pushes them to live and love with urgency. Whether you're a cancer patient or not, tomorrow is not promised. Act accordingly.

Wear the swimsuit.

Take the trip.

Write the book.

Start the business.

Love your people.

Love yourself.

Acknowledgements

During the early process of trying to write this book back in 2017, there were times when I felt the project was literally, physically fighting me. My body was sore. I found bruises and scratches on my skin that I couldn't explain, and I was always so tired. Jacob wrestled with an angel. I wrestled with words.

One day while taking a walk with my husband, he asked, "What is your book about exactly? I've been trying to tell people, but I can't. I don't have an elevator pitch." The problem was I didn't either. I realized writing this book had been so difficult because it lacked focus. The essays didn't have a common thread.

Then cancer happened.

Cancer happened and then I knew I wanted to publish a collection of essays about how you can write your way through anything. Cancer is an ugly disease, but it can show you just how beautiful people can be. So, I need to not only acknowledge people who helped make this book possible but also people who helped me get through the toughest year in my life because by doing so they helped make this book possible too.

To my Creator: You are my refuge. You are my restoration. You are my provider. You are my protector. Thank you for blessing me with the privilege of sharing my story, our story.

To my family: Mama, thank you for being my first best friend. Thank you for the paper dolls and Sanrio school supplies. Thank you for the Easy-Bake Oven and the tiny cakes we baked for Daddy. Thank you for making faux toast from milk cartons for my toy toaster. Thank you for showing me that love – just like writing – is all about the details. And thank you for never allowing illness to steal your smile or your laugh and for teaching me radical joy along the way. **Daddy**, thank you for always making me feel as if I'm smart enough to do anything and for instilling in me the work ethic needed to accomplish every goal I set – including writing this book. Thank you for letting me be a Daddy's girl no matter how old I get. **CJ**, thank you for being my calm before, during, and after every storm. You are my peace and the life of every party. #PowerToTheDreamers **Amanda**, thank you for loving my brother fiercely and for being the sister I've always wanted. And thank you for loving me enough to make me a custom Funko POP when I was going through treatment! **Teigan**, as

I write this you are just a few months old and I have yet to meet you. But I hope one day you'll grow up and read this book and know that being your auntie is a dream come true. **Kandis,** my "twin cousin" thank you for selflessly praying for me throughout my treatment even while you were walking through your own valley. **To the Bowsers and the Whites** – thank you for always making me feel like a part of your family.

To Tasha: Calling you my cousin or even my best friend has never felt sufficient. Even saying you're "like my sister" doesn't seem right. So, you need your own category. Thank you for every text – especially the ones you sent while I was sitting in the chemo chair. Thank you for responding to all of my texts – especially the ones about my book cover. Thank you for the headwraps, journals, t-shirts, Queasy Drops, and all the other gifts you sent me as I was going through treatment. Thank you for all the hilarious Instagram posts you sent to make sure cancer didn't cause me to forget how to laugh. Most of all thank you for never treating me like a sick person. For all these reasons and more you are my person.

To my friends: Mandy, thank you for being an editor for an early version of this book, for being such a vital part of the See Jane Write community, and for every time you've said you owe your writing success to me – even though I know you owe it to your talent and hard work. **Sherri**, thank you for being a beta reader for an early edition of this book and for being such a fantastic cheerleader for me and nearly everyone else in Birmingham. **Jennifer**, thank you for the walks and the talks and for inspiring me to follow in your footsteps down the self-publishing path. **Jessica**, I deeply admire how you use your voice to spread love and light and a spirit of acceptance, and you inspire me to do the same. **Kwoya**, thank you for making me go to therapy. You literally saved my life. Thank you for being a beta reader for an early version of this book and helping me calm down about the book cover process. Thank you for being the writer and the woman that you are. You always say I push you in the deep end, but you push me to higher heights. **Jacqui**, my sister in Beyoncé, you have an uncanny ability to push me to be better and do better while also inspiring me to love myself as is. Thank you. **Charlene**, you shine and light up everything and everyone around you – even from afar. You are my golden girl indeed. **Laura**, Edd calls you the unsung hero of my friend group. So let me sing your praises right now for every text and card you sent as I was going through treatment and for all the things in my life you made better from college to my summer in Seattle to my wedding day – just to name a few. **Mia W.,** you're like the younger sister I always wanted, and your big sis hopes you know how dope you are. **T. Marie**, Birmingham doesn't deserve you, but I hope you keep making us all better so that one day we will. **Glenny**, thank you for being my writing buddy, my TEDxBirmingham coach, and for encouraging me to apply for the Alabama State Council on the Arts fellowship that helped make this book possible. Thank you, Glenny, for making me brave. **April,** thank you for holding space for me in the Wildfire workshops, magazine, and community. And thank you for christening this book with your beautiful prose. **Geralyn**, even with oceans between us, our sisterhood remains intact forever. **Annemarie**, thank you for being the best work wife, for helping me be a better teacher, and for inspiring me to be a better person. To my **ASFA crew** – former classmates, former colleagues and former students – you are my family forever. // I would need another book to thank all of the friends who did something special for me during my treatment. Please know that I am grateful for you all.

To my Louisville loves: Birmingham is where I was born, but Louisville is where I became a woman, and it takes a village to raise a writer. There are so many people I met in River City who helped me grow into the woman and the writer I am today. Many of you have moved on to other cities, just as I have, but you'll always be my Louisville loves. Dahri, Amy, Glenn, Erika, Maisy, Lisa, Danielle, Diane, Tom, and Jim, thank you.

To the women of the See Jane Write community: I owe nearly every good thing that's happened in my writing life to you. And when cancer came burning through my world, you gave me beauty for ashes. Marie, you were my angel on earth helping me through every terrifying step of this so-called cancer journey. Mia P., after I announced my diagnosis, you took the time to write me a 3-page letter of encouragement that I cherished like scripture during my treatment. Coretta, thank you for helping me choose a fantastic surgeon, for the #seejavaciabeatcancer t-shirt, and for all the "canspiration" you've offered me and others. Karla, thanks for sending gift after gift during my treatment and for reminding me that even cancer can't stop me from being "Jayonce." Shirlene, thank you for your input on my book cover, for all you add to the See Jane Write community, and for giving me a glimpse of how fly I can be in my 60s and beyond. Carrie, you're the only person I know who seems to have each and every one of my quirks. So, thanks for your input on the cover and for the fact that each time I talk to you I feel less alone. Carla, thank you for teaching me that cancer ain't funny but we should laugh at it anyway. Audrey, thank you for sharing your publishing adventures with me, for being a loyal member of the See Jane Write community, and for being one of the funniest, most talented writers I know. Christina W., thank you for being you and for always reminding me that we write for freedom. Heidi, thank you for your support of the See Jane Write community through the years and for being a beta reader for an early version of this project. Chanda, thank you for being at the very first See Jane Write event and for everything you've done through the years to support this labor of love. // If you are a part of the See Jane Write community in any way, please know I am grateful for you and that this book is for you.

To the media outlets that helped me find my voice: From 2014 to 2018, I wrote a monthly column for *B-Metro* magazine in Birmingham. Many of the essays in this collection are expanded versions of pieces published there. I am forever grateful for the opportunity to share my story with B-Metro readers. A few essays are also revised versions of pieces I wrote for my "See Jane Write" column with Birmingham Magazine. And the ideas for other essays in this collection were birthed from pieces I wrote for Reckon South and the website for WBHM 90.3 FM – Birmingham's public radio station. Other media outlets I hold near and dear to my heart include *The Birmingham Times, The Courier-Journal, Good Grit magazine, StyleBlueprint, Babypalooza, HerMoney.com*, and *Wildfire* magazine.

To my publishing team: Dawn Michelle Hardy, The Literary Lobbyist -- thank you for being my guide on this publishing adventure. Latoya C. Smith, thank you for making my work stronger.

To my Beloved: Edward, when I say you are *everything* to me that is not cliché or hyperbole. You are more than my husband. You are my partner, my best friend, my spiritual guide, my healer, my teacher, my editor, my cheerleader and my coach. This book would not exist without you, without you pushing me to keep going, without you bringing me food during those marathon writing days, without you telling me again and again that women need my words. When you had to be my caregiver also and I would look at you with tears streaming down my face and say, "You didn't sign up for this," you'd reply, "Playa, I literally did," and somehow make me laugh on my darkest days. Marriage licenses and wedding vows aside, I do believe love is a decision. And choosing you was the best decision I've ever made. Thank you for choosing me again and again.

To my dear readers: Whether you've been rocking with me for years or you had no idea who I was before you picked up this book – I am grateful for you and I am rooting for you. My prayer is that this book has inspired you to write your story and share your truth.

Notes

F2020

1. "Best Songs of 2020," *The New York Times*, December 7, 2020. https://www.nytimes.com/2020/12/07/arts/music/best-songs.html
2. Kiara Collins. "Octavia Butler's personal journal shows the author literally wrote her life into existence," Blavity, January 28. 2016. https://blavity.com/octavia-butler/octavia-butler?category1=trending&category2=popular
3. Catherine Moore. "Positive Daily Affirmations: Is There Science Behind It?" *PositivePsychology.com*, March 16, 2021. https://positivepsychology.com/daily-affirmations/

How Does a Feminist Fight Cancer?

1. Chimamanda Ngozi Adichie. "We Should All Be Feminists," TED, December 2012. https://www.ted.com/talks/chimamanda_ngozi_adichie_we_should_all_be_feminists
2. "Feminism," *Merriam-Webster.com*. https://www.merriam-webster.com/dictionary/feminism

Sisterhood of the Traveling Pens

1. Natalie Goldberg. *Writing Down the Bones* (Boston: Shambhala, 1986).

Jesus Is My Homeboy

1. Sarah Bessey. *Jesus Feminist* (New York: Howard Books, 2013).
2. Matthew 22:36-40, The Holy Bible, New International Version.
3. Matthew 18:3, The Holy Bible, New International Version.

Cancer Is a Cruel Teacher

1. Elaine Welteroth, *More Than Enough.* (New York: Viking, 2019).

Ain't I a Feminist?

1. Hal Boedeker, "Burns Turns To Anthony and Stanton," The Orlando Sentinel, November 7, 1999. https://www.orlandosentinel.com/news/os-xpm-1999-11-07-9911050417-story.html
2. Nsenga K. Burton. "These 19 black women fought for voting rights," USA Today, February 8, 2020. https://www.usatoday.com/story/life/womenofthecentury/2020/02/08/black-history-month-these-19-black-women-fought-voting-rights/2842276001/
3. Tamara Winfrey Harris. "All Hail the Queen?" *Bitch*, May 20, 2013. https://www.bitchmedia.org/article/all-hail-the-queen-beyonce-feminism
4. "Rediscovering History: The 100th Anniversary of the Ratification of the 19th Amendment, *StyleBlueprint*, August 13, 2020. https://styleblueprint.com/everyday/19th-amendment-ratification-100th-anniversary/
5. Michelle Harris. "10 Black Suffragists You Should Know," *Mental Floss*, August 18, 2020. https://www.mentalfloss.com/article/626809/black-suffragists-you-should-know
6. Rachel Hartigan. "A century after women's suffrage, the fight for equality isn't over," *National Geographic*, July 21, 2020. https://www.nationalgeographic.com/magazine/article/a-century-after-womens-suffrage-the-fight-for-equality-isnt-over-feature
7. Anna North. "The 19th Amendment didn't give women the right to vote," *Vox*, August 18, 2020. https://www.vox.com/2020/8/18/21358913/19th-amendment-ratified-anniversary-women-suffrage-vote
8. Nick Fouriezos. "Gloria Steinem: Black Women Drove the Feminist Movement," OZY, October 2, 2020. https://www.ozy.com/news-and-politics/gloria-steinem-black-women-drove-the-feminist-movement/381923/
9. "11 Black Women Who Helped Shape Gloria Steinem & The Second-Wave Feminist Movement," Broadway Box Daily Scoop, February 28, 2019. https://www.broadwaybox.com/daily-scoop/11-black-women-influenced-shape-gloria-steinem/

Why I Won't Shut Up about Being a Girl–or Being Black

1. Kenya Hunt. *Girl Gurl Grrrl: On Womanhood and Belonging in the Age of Black Girl Magic.* (New York: Amistad, 2020).
2. Linda Chavers. "Why I Don't Love #BlackGirlMagic," Elle, January 13, 2016. https://www.elle.com/life-love/a33180/why-i-dont-love-blackgirlmagic/
3. Demetria Lucas. "Elle, You Just Don't Understand #BlackGirlMagic," *The Root,* January 14, 2016. https://www.theroot.com/elle-you-just-don-t-understand-blackgirlmagic-1790853913

I'm Feeling Lucky – and Enraged

1. "Everything You Should Know About Breast Cancer in Your 20s and 30s," Healthline.com, November 13,2019. https://www.healthline.com/health/breast-cancer/breast-cancer-20s-30s
2. Clement. G. Yedjou et al. "Health and Racial Disparity in Breast Cancer," January 3, 2020. https://www.ncbi.nlm.nih.gov/pmc/articles/PMC6941147/
3. Christen Linke Young. "There are clear, race-based inequalities in health insurance and health outcomes," Brookings, February 19, 2020. https://www.brookings.edu/blog/usc-brookings-schaeffer-on-health-policy/2020/02/19/there-are-clear-race-based-inequalities-in-health-insurance-and-health-outcomes/
4. Kelly M. Hoffman, et al. "Racial bias in pain assessment and treatment recommendations, and false beliefs about biological differences between blacks and whites," Proceedings of the National Academy of Sciences of the United States of America, April 19, 2016. https://www.pnas.org/content/113/16/4296
5. "Working Together to Reduce Black Maternal Mortality," CDC. https://www.cdc.gov/healthequity/features/maternal-mortality/index.html
6. Black Maternal Health Momnibus. Learn more: https://blackmaternalhealthcaucus-underwood.house.gov/Momnibus
7. Hear Her Campaign. CDC. Learn more: https://www.cdc.gov/hearher/indcx.html
8. Tigerlily Foundation. Learn more: https://www.tigerlilyfoundation.org/

This Is What a Feminist Writer Looks Like

1. Julia Gazdag. "Feminist or Feminine? Oh Wait, They Aren't Mutually Exclusive," Hello Giggles, April 2, 2013. https://hellogiggles.com/lifestyle/feminist-or-feminine-oh-wait-they-arent-mutually-exclusive/
2. Chimamanda Ngozi Adichie. "We Should All Be Feminists," TED, December 2012. https://www.ted.com/talks/chimamanda_ngozi_adichie_we_should_all_be_feminists

On Walking and Writing

1. Duncan Minshull. *Beneath My Feet: Writers on Walking* (Notting Hill Editions, 2018).
2. Henry David Thoreau. "Walking," *The Atlantic*, June 1862. https://www.theatlantic.com/magazine/archive/1862/06/walking/304674/
3. "Journaling for Mental Health," University of Rochester Medical Center. https://www.urmc.rochester.edu/encyclopedia/content.aspx?ContentID=4552&ContentTypeID=1
4. "Why walking is the most underrated form of exercise," NBCNews.com, September 2, 2017. https://www.nbcnews.com/better/health/why-walking-most-underrated-form-exercise-ncna797271
5. Jane Chertoff. "What Are the Benefits of Walking," Healthline.com, November 8, 2018. https://www.healthline.com/health/benefits-of-walking
6. Marily Oppezzo and Daniel L. Schwartz. Give Your Ideas Some Legs: The Positive Effect of Walking on Creative Thinking, Journal of Experimental Psychology, 2014. https://www.apa.org/pubs/journals/releases/xlm-a0036577.pdf
7. May Wong. "Stanford study finds walking improves creativity, Stanford News, April 24, 2014. https://news.stanford.edu/2014/04/24/walking-vs-sitting-042414/

Body Paragraphs

1. "What Is Lupus?" Lupus Foundation of America. https://www.lupus.org/resources/what-is-lupus
2. "Lupus facts and statistics," Lupus Foundation of America. https://www.lupus.org/resources/lupus-facts-and-statistics
3. Emily C. Somers, et al. Population-Based Incidence and Prevalence of Systemic Lupus Erythematosus, Arthritis Rheumatol, February 2014. https://www.ncbi.nlm.nih.gov/pmc/articles/PMC4198147/

Proud to Be a Southern Fried Feminist

1. Amanda Hooper. "Let's Talk About Intersectional Feminism, National Women's Law Center, November 4, 2015. https://nwlc.org/blog/lets-talk-about-intersectional-feminism/
2. Rich Benjamin. "My road trip through the whitest towns in America," TEDWomen, 2015. https://www.ted.com/talks/rich_benjamin_my_road_trip_through_the_whitest_towns_in_america

Birmingham – You Don't Get to Hate It Unless You Love It

1. Natalie Goldberg. *Writing Down the Bones* (Boston: Shambhala, 1986).

Home Is Where Your Story Is

1. Michelle Obama. *Becoming* (New York: Crown Publishing, 2018).

The New New Year's Eve

1. Lucille Clifton. "won't you celebrate with me," Book of Light (Port Townsend: Copper Canyon Press, 1993). https://www.poetryfoundation.org/poems/50974/wont-you-celebrate-with-me

About the Author

Javacia Harris Bowser is an award-winning freelance journalist and the founder of See Jane Write, which a friend of hers once called "the Sisterhood of the Traveling Pens." See Jane Write is a website and community for women who write and blog that Javacia founded in 2011 in her hometown of Birmingham, Alabama. Today, See Jane Write serves and brings together women from across the country and around the world. Named one of Birmingham's Top 40 Under 40, Javacia believes we can all write our way to the life of our dreams – a message she often conveys to the women of See Jane Write. When she was diagnosed with breast cancer in 2020, she learned how to write her way through her worst nightmare, too.

Javacia was included in *Southern Living* magazine's list of Innovators Changing the South, alongside household names like Dolly Parton and Reese Witherspoon, and is a recipient of the 2022 Alabama State Council on the Arts Fellowship. With a focus on women's lifestyle, wealth, and wellness, Javacia has written for a number of local, regional, and national media outlets including *USA Today*, Business Insider, HerMoney.com, *Good Grit* magazine, and *The Birmingham Times*. In 2020, her column for *Birmingham* magazine was awarded Best Magazine Column by the Alabama Press Association. Javacia is a proud graduate of the journalism programs at the University of Alabama and the University of California at Berkeley. When she isn't writing, you can find Javacia reading books, eating tacos, listening to Beyoncé, or spending time with her husband Edward.